NEW ME█████████
IN PUB███
RELATIONS

THE EVOLVING SCENARIO IN INDIA

TOMOJIT BHATTACHARJEE

INDIA · SINGAPORE · MALAYSIA

Notion Press

No. 8, 3rd Cross Street,
CIT Colony, Mylapore,
Chennai, Tamil Nadu - 600 004

First Published by Notion Press 2020
Copyright © Tomojit Bhattacharjee 2020
All Rights Reserved.

ISBN 978-1-64919-553-1

Dedicated to
Maa Baba

Contents

Preface

New media tools which involve the use of a number of new age internet based platforms such as websites, social media, mobile applications etc. have completely rewritten the rules of communication today. For decades, the mainstream media such as print, much later radio and television, had held the position of being the gatekeepers of information for the society.

However, new media has completely changed that dynamic. Now, any individual, government or corporate entity can disseminate information to the public through these platforms. They do not have to rely on the newspapers or electronic media to get their view or information across.

The sphere of public relations has also adjusted its strategies accordingly. There was a time when the bulk of a public relations campaign used to rely on conventional media platforms such as print and electronic. However, in the last few years, that arrangement has changed. Now, online visibility, social media traction and engagement form very crucial components of any public relations campaign or strategy.

While this change started making its presence felt on the corporate scene pretty early around the beginning of the last decade, the Indian public sector did not adopt these strategies straightaway. A handful of government institutions and organizations which were actually employing these tools were getting greatly benefitted. Therefore, to study the potential, that the employment of new media tools could have on the public relations strategies of the Indian public sector, I started my doctoral research back in 2011.

The findings of my research pointed out the many benefits that employment of new media could have on the government sector. The study found that new media could not only increase efficiency but could also improve the image that the government establishments had in front of the people. In my study, I took up the Delhi Traffic Police as one of the case studies and found that their social media handles and accounts were hugely successful in presenting the force as a committed and humane entity, which cared for the people.

Subsequently, since 2014, it can be noticed that the central government led by Sh. Narendra Modi has focused a great deal towards the employment of new media tools in their publicity strategies. Today, every prominent political figure, ministry, department or public sector establishment has presence on all new media platforms. Almost, every piece of information is shared through social media on a regular basis.

This book focuses overall on how the domain of public relations is getting benefitted from new media. The book separately analyses how new media has influenced public relations strategies in the private as well as the public sectors. It takes up interesting case studies both in the government and the private sectors to show, how public relations as a profession is gradually changing because of the onslaught of new media.

The book also makes an attempt to analyze the evolving dimensions of new media such as influencer marketing, social media algorithms etc. In one of the chapters, an attempt has been made to study the apprehension that the entire new media domain is like a bubble, which would eventually burst and the world would go back to its conventional, tried and tested methods of communication.

A lot of content in the book have been adopted from my doctoral research work, which I had completed back in 2015. However, since this field is very dynamic, I have tried to add new elements and developments after studying the sector thoroughly.

This book will also be of great benefit to the students who are pursuing Bachelors or Masters courses in Mass Communication in general or Public Relations in particular. On a relatively recent topic like new media, publications are not easily available. Most of the times, students and researchers have to rely on the material that is available online. With this particular publication, they will have the option of a book, which I would also try to update and enhance further in the subsequent editions.

Tomojit Bhattacharjee

Acknowledgements

Any publication, big or small, fructifies only because of the cooperation, guidance and encouragement extended to the author by some people. This book is also no different. I would like to take this opportunity to thank my parents, Ranjita and Tanmay Bhattacharjee and my wife Nitu for their continuous encouragement and support.

I would also like to express my gratitude to my guides during the doctoral research, Prof. Gyan Prakash Pandey and Prof. Silajit Guha for motivating me to take up this study. I would remain ever indebted to my boss, Mr. Anuj Dayal, Executive Director, Corporate Communications at DMRC and all my colleagues for allowing me to spare time for this effort despite our busy work schedules.

My sister, Srijani and brother in law, Shantanu always guided me in the right direction, while my in laws, Sati and Sushil Chakraborty as well as my brother in law Venketeshwar and his wife Madhuri extended a lot of logistical support during the research. The kids in the family, my little son Nirjhar and my adorable nieces Doyal and Siya also deserve a special mention for all the positivity they spread during this journey. Last but certainly not the least, I thank my friends Amit, Sandipan, Samrat, Bidyut and Uttam for their timely help and inputs.

Tomojit Bhattacharjee

New Media – A View of the Studies Already Conducted

Even though the use of new media tools in the sphere of media in general and public relations in particular, are a recent phenomenon, there have been many studies analysing the role and scope of new media in the world of media as a whole.

However, before we proceed towards studying the literature that has been generated to analyse the role of new media in the world of media as well as in public relations, let us take a look at some definitions of the term new media and its usage in relation to the other recently coined term 'social media'.

"New Media is a 21st Century catchall term used to define all that is related to the internet and the interplay between technology, images and sound. In fact, the definition of new media changes daily, and will continue to do so. New media evolves and morphs continuously. What it will be tomorrow is virtually unpredictable for most of us, but we do know that it will continue to evolve in fast and furious ways." (Socha and Eber-Schmid, 2012)

"New media doesn't necessarily refer to a specific mode of communication. Some types of new media, such as an online newspaper, are also "old media" in the form of a traditional printed newspaper. Other new media are entirely new, such as a podcast or smartphone app. It becomes even more complicated to define when you consider that as technology continues to advance, the definition continually changes.

New media is any media – from newspaper articles and blogs to music and podcasts – that are delivered digitally. From a website or email to mobile phones and streaming apps, any internet-related form of communication can be considered new media." (Kote, 2020)

In the recent times, the terms new media and social media have often been used to explain the same thing. On many occasions, they are also used intermittently for each other. "Not all media is social. Media becomes social when you can interact with the content via comments or conversation. While old media was a passive form of entertainment, new media is interactive entertainment or edutainment. Social media, on the other hand requires a conversation between the content creator/s and the audience. Social media is about the people who engage on the platform. If people are connecting through the media, then it is social.

Basically, social media is a subset of new media, but not all new media is social. In order for new media to be considered social, it needs to have an element of interactivity where the audience can contribute, connect or collaborate with the content. On Twitter, the audience can share your content or talk with the content producer. Instagram allows followers to comment on, share and like photos. Blogs can be social and invite conversation in the comments or they can turn comments off and just create new media. Comments, likes and the ability to share content make media social. Other phrases for social media or new media are digital media, interactive media and user generated media". (Michaelian, 2012)

Therefore, from the above studies, we can conclude that social media is an integral part of new media and gives new media an interactive perspective. Initially let us analyse the studies that have been conducted to focus on the impact made by new media tools in the world of media as a whole.

Canadian Research Firm, FAD Research, in a study titled, "Changing Media, Changing Roles: New Media Comes of Age" had mentioned about the role of the new media tools in changing the overall media landscape of the world way back in the year 2006.

"Media consumption is gravitating towards increased use of interactive platforms that are not tied to a single location or confined to the display of a single type of media. Media programming is being promoted and distributed across a wider array of platforms.

Consumers are headed towards reaching a state of ultramedia, a condition whereby all media is accessible at any time from any location. Media production is no longer a business that occurs in discrete silos as producers need to consider the array of channels open to them to reach an audience. Conducting regulation of the media environment has become increasingly complex (and irrelevant). Traditional media packagers and distributors continue to be disintermediated as producers find new ways to go directly to market." (FAD Research, 2006)

Christine Larabie, in a study titled, "A Reflection on the Role of New Media – From Peer-to-Peer to Protest" also recognises that new media is enabling more participation by the audience. "Participation is also a widely used term, especially in the context of new media technologies that enable peer-to-peer file sharing, and encourage users to actively create and distribute content. This participation is believed to have widened social spheres and revitalized political communication, addressing many problems associated with traditional media." (Larabie, 2011)

Researchers also feel that gradually new and traditional media tools are assimilating with each other and contributing positively towards the overall media landscape. For example, during the popular uprisings in many Arab countries in 2011, also known as the Arab spring, new media tools played a major role towards ensuring the freedom of speech.

"It is increasingly difficult to separate new media from old media. In the Arab Spring, the two reinforced each other. New media must be understood as part of a wider information arena in which new and old media form complex interrelationships.

An extraordinary wave of popular protest swept the Arab world in 2011. Massive popular mobilization brought down long-ruling leaders in Tunisia and Egypt, helped spark bloody struggles in Bahrain, Libya, Syria, and Yemen, and fundamentally reshaped the nature of politics in the region. Internet-based social media such as Twitter, Facebook, and YouTube played a visible role in many of these movements, especially for foreign audiences experiencing the turmoil vicariously through real-time Twitter feeds or YouTube videos posted to Facebook pages." (Aday, Farrell, Lynch, Sides and Freelon, 2011)

In countries where the freedom of press is not guaranteed, new media tools are playing a role in transforming the media scenario. Peruvian freelance journalist Yvette Sierra Praeli, in her paper titled, "New Media and the Freedom of Press" says that new media bypasses government restrictions on freedom of the press in countries like Iran, Cuba and China.

"Even though internet access is controlled and restricted in these countries, people have found different ways to avoid state control. They use blogs, Twitter, Facebook, Youtube and other social media to express themselves. But they have to find different mechanisms to be able to upload their posts in their own blogs." (Praeli, 2011)

Among the research works that focus on the role of internet in public relations, one interesting study undertaken in the United States in 2007 recognized the huge scope of internet in devising public relations strategies. "The Internet gives public relations practitioners a unique opportunity to collect information, monitor public opinion on issues, and engage in direct dialogue with their publics about a variety of issues". (McAllister & Taylor, 2007)

Much earlier in 1999, American researcher Lisa Hoggatt of the San Jose State University, in a thesis had also mentioned about the immense potential of new media technology, then perceived only as the internet, as a tool of public relations.

"New media technology is rapidly evolving the media industry and the practices of mass communications. New media technology is the application of digital (computer) technology to mass communications. In a few short years, two main factors associated with the technology have changed the media landscape. The Internet emerged as a communication medium. Even though the Internet is still in its infancy, its impact on society, commerce, and the government is already phenomenal. In addition, the interactivity and immediacy inherent in digital technology have changed the models of media production and business for all media". (Hoggatt, 1999)

Kirk Hallahan, a Professor of Mass Communication at the Colorado State University also had recognised the tremendous potential of the internet in the domain of public relations, way back in a study conducted in the year 2004, "It has dramatically changed the way public relations practitioners distribute information, interact with key publics, deal with crises, and manage issues". (Hallahan, 2004)

"Social networking enables instant sharing of information and, as the number of people using the Internet continues to rise, with many blogging themselves, releases you post can be easily picked up and posted by other bloggers and online journalists. This offers you wider coverage of your news and ensures it reaches a larger target audience." (www.vitispr.com, 2020)

To analyse the immense capability of the internet as a disseminator of information, G.H Alfonso and S. Smith, in their article, "Crisis communications management on the web: how internet-based technologies are changing the way public relations professionals handle crisis" published in the Journal of Contingencies and Crisis Management in 2008 cite the example of the US based company, Kryptonite locks, about which, a small blog called www.bikeforums.net published a post stating that one of Kryptonite's bike locks could be opened using a pen.

Within five days of this post, the news was taken up by a popular blog called 'Engadget'. The news of the faulty locks soon spread all over the Internet and then found its way to the conventional media. Kryptonite initially ignored the blog, but later realized that they had a major crisis to deal with. (Alfonso and Smith, 2008)

Research has also shown that public relations practitioners who embrace new technologies such as blogging are perceived within organisations as having more power, in that they are willing to be leaders in the industry and use new tools to better reach target publics (Porter, Sweetser Trammell, Chung, & Kim, 2007).

An analysis sheds considerable light on the potential of social networking sites, particularly Twitter. "Twitter can do so much more than help you "push" messages and content. When used effectively as tool for listening and monitoring, Twitter can be a lens through which you can observe the flow of information and culture. You can not only receive information, you'll also perceive where information came from, where it's going, and where it might go tomorrow." (Gordon, 2011)

American public relations professional James L. Horton, in an article titled "PR and Social Media" writes that "Newspapers are withering. Network television has watched audiences decline. Radio is splintered. Magazines are shrinking. Meanwhile, there are millions of bloggers and Facebook users, Twitterers and texters and Linked-in businesspeople. As reporters disappear from traditional media, PR practitioners are forced to consider and to use social media". (Horton, 2009)

Many studies globally have mentioned in details about the benefits of social media in the sphere of public relations. Brad Smith, in an article titled "Why Social Media is the new public relations" published in the Fixcourse newsletter opines, "Social media dramatically lowers the cost of customer acquisition, and increases the lifetime value of a customer exponentially".

"It also has the added bonus of being inherently viral, which means that when you reach a certain point, your customers will do your marketing for you. Each new customer will bring one or two customers of their own, simply through recommendations."

"One of the biggest advantages of social media is that it allows you to have a two-way discussion with people. This helps you to create a bond, and makes sure they remain happy customers," he further mentions. (Smith, 2011)

Indian public relations professional Varghese Thomas, in an article titled, "How is Social Media Evolving PR" also writes about the manner in which new media is changing the profession of public relations. "In the early days, the internet consisted of one-way communications in the form of static websites and two-way communication through email. Over the past several years, the internet has grown to be the most premiere medium for two-way or multi-way conversations which changed the dynamics of Public Relations (PR). Just a few of examples include social interaction through Facebook, tagging in Technorati or Digg, and micro-blogging sites like Twitter.

Let's take a step back and see how PR used to operate. Old timers in the PR industry woke up most mornings to craft a press release and then left it to the mailroom boys to send it out to editors. To hasten the process, fax machines were used. Towards the late 1990s e-mail became an alternative delivery method. The press release went as an attachment. The smarter set began to create landing pages for journalists on their websites that had announcements and releases, downloadable pictures and logos. How cool was that?

Today's PR professionals wake up to an entirely different scenario. There's social media to contend with. It's not just broadcast; its multi-media, images, tags, keywords, links, listening to your target audience and engaging them in conversations. Press releases must still go out. Journalists must continue to be on the PR professional's A-list. But all that is turning into Old School PR. Even traditional websites now include user-generated content options like ratings, comments, forums and reviews. These sites have been enthusiastically accepted by the public, while search engines have recently begun to share real-time news and Twitter results about many hot topics. Cumulatively, this type of multi-way online communication is referred to as social media." (Thomas, 2012)

Social media website www.maximisesocialmedia.com, claims that an overwhelming majority of public relations practitioners today use the social media for their professional requirements. "A recent survey found that an eye-opening 80% of public relations professionals routinely use social media to cultivate media relationships, share important company news and solicit feedback. Perhaps even more importantly, clients and business affiliations are turning to social media as a primary source of news and information about products, services or other updates of interest." (www. maximisesocialmedia.com, 2012)

Focusing on the increasing use of social media as a marketing and communication tool in India, Indian social media monitoring blog, www.socialsamosa.com asserts that the country's corporates are now using social media more and more as it's an easy yet effective way to reach the target audience.

"With the growing acceptance of the social media space in India, brands have accepted social media as an important part of their marketing communication strategies." (www. socialsamosa.com, 2012)

Another important aspect of social or new media as a tool of public relations is that their effectiveness or popularity can be conveniently assessed, therefore, facilitating the easy redrawing of strategies if required. Sites such as www.indiadigitalreview.com take up such studies in a neutral manner periodically. Corporates also have their own internal assessment mechanisms to analyse the outcomes of their social media campaigns.

The social networking sites such as Facebook, Twitter and Linkdin have communities dedicated to the public relations practitioners of India. Media movements, Public Relations India are examples of a few such communities on Facebook. Media Mimansa, a journal on Mass Communication brought out by the Makhan Lal Chaturvedi University, Bhopal also features some in-depth articles on new media from time to time.

www.indiaprblog.com is another website which has some interesting case studies on PR practices submitted by PR professionals. On the use of digital media, one such post says, "Often for our clients, we most of the time try to integrate digital support to PR and marketing activities. It appears that to pull off really big digital campaigns, it is now time for the other way round. Big bang digital idea, which has its heart on the web, is executed well online and supported by offline mass media, and of course, it is supported by mobile phone marketing as well. For instance, a simple online contest can grow many folds when we add in an element of receiving the entries through SMS or voice calls." (Ningthoujam, 2009).

In a well researched article in the Financial Express in 2009, Lakshmipathy Bhatt wrote, "In a first of its kind, TataSky has experimented with a Twitter-enabled advertising banner to promote Tata Sky Active. Tata Motors successfully created hype and garnered test drive bookings prior to the launch of Indigo Manza through a social media campaign. There are several other brands using the digital medium as a critical part of their marketing mix. These are exciting times in the digital advertising space". (Bhatt, 2009) This clearly shows that digital media, which is almost another name for new media, was becoming an integral part of the overall marketing strategies of the Indian corporate world by the start of the decade of 2010s.

Commenting about the potential of social media and public relations, eminent public relations expert Deirdre Breakenridge says, "India will experience a great deal of growth in the area of PR and social media, as the Internet and technology continue to become more essential to businesses. We have already seen heavy usage of social media participation on Facebook, Twitter and LinkedIn. PR professionals in India will be required to expand their knowledge, skills and communication practices as consumers and business come to rely more on social media communities to deliver communications and to engage with the public. Although PR doesn't own social media, because it is proliferating worldwide, we need to be able to breakdown the communication opportunities for our brands, and also be able to counsel and measure results." (www.text100.com)

Many researchers also feel that social media creates more opportunities for the upholding of the freedom of press. "New media hold great potential as a resource for press freedom and freedom of expression. They serve as a platform for dialogue across borders and allow for innovative approaches to the distribution and acquisition of knowledge. These qualities are vital to press freedom. But they may be undercut by attempts to regulate and censor both access and content."

There have been many studies which have tried to analyse the paradigm shift that new media is bringing in the sphere of journalism. Now, the journalist is not the only disseminator of news to the society. There are many other alternative media to do that. "The venerable profession of journalism finds itself at a rare moment in history where, for the first time, its hegemony as gatekeeper of the news is threatened by not just new technology and competitors but, potentially, by the audience it serves. Armed with easy-to-use Web publishing tools, always-on connections and increasingly powerful mobile devices, the online audience has the means to become an active participant in the creation and dissemination of news and information" (Bowman and Willis, 2003)

Chapter 1

Growth and Development of the Public Relations Industry in India

In simple language, Public Relations can be defined as the process of communicating with the key stakeholders in an effective manner to ensure that the desired information that is required to be conveyed is successfully communicated. Over the years, public relations has matured to become an industry marshaled by professionals. However, about a century ago, it was not considered worthy of being recognized as a separate industry.

"Public Relations is the creation, distribution and dissemination of messaging and communications for the purpose of promoting and fostering positive awareness, associations, imagery, perception of a person, place or thing among a particular target audience to effect a desired behavior". (Gersten. D, Heidi Cohen Actionable Marketing Guide, www.heidicohen.com, 2011)

Public Relations as an independent industry flourished in the 1990s after the liberalization of the Indian economy. As more and more firms entered the Indian market in different spheres of businesses, the need to liaison with the media and maintain a healthy public image became important.

"The public relations industry of India today (2019) is worth about Rs. 1,600 crores with more than a thousand independent public relations agencies functioning in different parts of the country. All major corporate entities also have extensive public relations or corporate communications machineries who have a say in almost all important activities of the organization starting from the very selection of a new product or service to its eventual launch in the market.

The public relations (PR) industry grew 12 per cent to touch Rs 1,600 crore in FY19, according to the fourth 'State of the Industry Survey 2019' report by the Public Relations Consultants Association of India (PRCAI). While media relations continue to be the largest service, non-media relations services now contribute 53 per cent of the industry's revenue.

The online survey, conducted among 34 PR companies in India between July and August 2019 by i2iResearch, has forecast that the industry will continue to grow at a CAGR of 12.5 per cent, reaching Rs 1,800 crore by 2020. " (www. adgully.com, 2019)

The growth of the public relations industry in the country has been gradual. The Tata Group was the first ever corporate house to establish a separate public relations department in 1943. The department initially started with an internal publication for the employees. However, till the 1990s, the sector practically remained unorganized. Some advertising agencies had PR arms, which offered PR services in addition to the advertising campaigns. Some international PR firms, like Ogilvy PR did set shop in the mid 80s but there was no proliferation of such agencies as such. Similarly, some local PR firms were also set up across different parts of the country without much significant success.

"India didn't have an official public relations body until 11 years after the independence, when the Public Relations Society of India (PRSI) was established. The organization was meant to formally regulate the public relations profession for the first time in India. When the country started to witness globalization in the early 1990s, public relations recognized its right place for the first time. With foreign investment, a growing economy, and the emergence of multinational corporations, the value and public perception of brands suddenly started to matter. As a result, PR took a different shape altogether.

During this time, global agencies, like Ogilvy & Mather, opened offices in India. Since then the PR industry in India began to observe a remarkable evolution. In the 2000s, the industry watched further growth when the New York-based Burson-Marsteller, one of the largest global public relations firms in the world, acquired the Indian public relation company Genesis, which was founded in the 90s. Gradually, the Indian PR industry is receiving more and more attention for creating innovative strategic communications, building significant brands, dealing with crisis and improving customer communication." (Banerjee, P., 2017)

The public relations apparatus in the corporate world is primarily divided into two verticals. On one side are the public relations agencies, which are specialized in handling media relations and other ancillary services and on the other are the Corporate Communication professionals who are employed by the corporates directly for handling the same requirements. Presently, most major corporates have a limited number of communications professionals. However, they hire the PR agencies for handling their communication needs. So, the corporate communication professionals primarily liaison with the agency people for the management of the communication requirements.

This arrangement has now become the norm. Initially, prior to globalization in the 1990s, major corporate houses in the country had their own communication set ups as the agency PR industry was still in its infancy. However, with PR agencies, now springing up, most corporate entities recruit only a minimum number of people and then hire an agency. Many smaller establishments do not recruit their own staff at all and rely on the agencies for all their publicity related requirements.

Over the years, the public relations industry has also diversified into various specialized areas. For example, many PR firms now have separate digital media arms, which primarily handle the digital requirements of companies. Under the digital media purview, a range of activities such as social media management, website and mobile app handling, blog maintenance etc are included. Over the last decade, various independent digital media agencies have also sprung up which offer end to end digital media solutions to the clients.

However, interestingly, public relations existed as an arm of the government agencies much before the private sector realized its potential. The Press Information Bureau (PIB) was created by the colonial rulers way back in 1919 even before the independence of the country.

"In the old British days, the organization (PIB) came into being as the Bureau of Public Information (BPI). The name was a little inappropriate inasmuch as the Bureau was not conceived as an office where the public could get information on the doings of a foreign government. The colonial rulers were often secretive but some high-minded persons who manned the set- up in the earlier days were bold enough to think of serving the Press in a proper manner.

The BPI, no doubt, performed its task under the colonial rule well. Then came Independence and the Government of free India saw quickly the value of a centralised agency to service the Press. In those days only the print media mattered. But soon the radio effectively voiced the feelings of a newly independent people and the definition of the Press went on changing." (Bhatt, 2000)

The Press Information Bureau today is one of the biggest sources of information for the Indian media with 39 regional as well as branch offices across the country, with the headquarter in New Delhi. PIB has more than 1,400 accredited journalists based in Delhi including many foreign correspondents from prestigious publications.

The Public Sector Undertakings generally have dedicated departments to handle the public relations responsibilities with an officer of the rank of general manager handling it. In the current scenario, the top Maharatna PSUs would have an annual public relations budget of around a hundred crores, However, the importance given to the public relations departments of the PSUs often depend on the attitude of the top management. If the top executive or the board of directors are media savvy, the PR apparatus gets a lot of work, if they are not, then the PR people end up doing very little apart from printing leaflets and brochures.

In the states, the directorates of information and publicity, more or less work on the pattern of the PIB. They have officers attached to the ministries and departments and every district has a district level public relation officer. The department is generally headed by a senior state service or IAS officer.

With the passage of time, the role and nature of work of these public sector professionals under the government has tremendously changed. Even a couple of decades back, the independent media landscape of the country primarily consisted of a few newspapers and magazines only. The radio and the television services available in India, i.e, the All India Radio (AIR) and Doordarshan were both state owned. Internet had not yet made its foray into the offices and bedrooms of the nation yet.

Therefore, quite obviously the media relations activities of those times were rather limited or minimal in comparison to the highly demanding scenario now when the 24X7 news environment compels public relations professionals of all spheres, either private or government to respond to their queries almost immediately. The primary activity of the public relations officers was to bring out literatures such as brochures, leaflets, hoardings etc conveying the details of the projects taken up by the government.

They would also be required to set up stalls during various fairs, exhibitions and conclaves for the same purpose. In addition, these public relations officials were seen as smooth talkers who had the necessary connections to make logistical arrangements such as flight bookings, hotel accommodations etc apart from entertaining clients, guests, VIPs etc during official meetings and seminars. Many of these government run public relations departments also have dedicated archive sections which record most of the important government events through photographs as well as video records.

The Government of India launched the 'Digital India' programme in the year 2015. Since then, there has been a major thrust on digitizing government services and taking them directly to the people. The domain of communication has also not remained immune to this phenomenon. India's Prime Minister, Sh. Narendra Modi joined Twitter in January, 2009 much before he assumed the role of the Prime Minister. Since 2014, after he took charge, there has been a lot of focus on use of new media tools for communication of the government's policies and initiatives to the people. In the subsequent chapters, we shall analyse these aspects in details.

Public Relations education has also become more structured over the years. In the year 1960, a course on PR was organized by Tata Steel under the purview of the Calcutta Management Association. In 1981, the Indian Institute of Mass Communication, started a Post Graduate Diploma in Advertising and Public Relations. Gradually, all Journalism departments across colleges and universities in the country started including Public Relations as a separate subject. Today, a number of government as well as private institutions across the country provide diploma courses specializing in Public Relations.

Therefore, to sum up, we may say that, the profession of public relations has evolved a great deal over the last few decades. Till the 1990s, the sector was largely static with limited activity as an organized sector. However, globalization opened the floodgates and many public relations agencies emerged to cater to the communication requirements of the companies which were setting shop in India under the changed economic environment. The onslaught of cable television, entry of the internet and then the advent of the new media era has further enhanced the importance of this sector. These are indeed exciting times for the Public Relations professionals!!

Chapter 2

New Media – Concept and Definitions

"New Media is a 21st Century catchall term used to define all that is related to the internet and the interplay between technology, images and sound. In fact, the definition of new media changes daily, and will continue to do so. New media evolves and morphs continuously. What it will be tomorrow is virtually unpredictable for most of us, but we do know that it will continue to evolve in fast and furious ways." (Socha B., Eber-Schmid b, 2012)

From the above mentioned definition of the term 'New Media', it can be deciphered that it is a rather broad term which encompasses almost all the new age innovations that have taken place in the domain of communications. Coming out from the audio – visual era when television and radio were regarded as the zenith of communicative success by mankind, we have now moved towards a world woven by the internet. The barriers of geography have been breached like never before and the world today can be seen by the press of a button on our mobile phones. The revolution in the telecommunication sector also has been exemplary and therefore, most new innovations in the world of communication are witnessing a marriage between the world of internet and mobile telephony.

To understand the world of new media in greater details, let us analyse how the sector evolved gradually. The first and foremost pillar of the 'new media' paradigm was undoubtedly the internet, since it facilitated the instantaneous communication of thoughts and ideas to a large audience with the potential for immediate feedback at a reasonable cost.

"The first recorded description of the social interactions that could be enabled through networking was a series of memos written by J.C.R. Licklider of MIT in August 1962 discussing his "Galactic Network" concept. Licklider was the first head of the computer research program at DARPA, starting in October 1962. While at DARPA* he convinced his successors at DARPA, Ivan Sutherland, Bob Taylor, and MIT researcher Lawrence G. Roberts, of the importance of this networking concept.

Leonard Kleinrock at MIT published the first paper on packet switching theory in July 1961 and the first book on the subject in 1964. Kleinrock convinced Roberts of the theoretical feasibility of communications using packets rather than circuits, which was a major step along the path towards computer networking.

In late 1966 Roberts went to DARPA to develop the computer network concept and quickly put together his plan for the "ARPANET"*, publishing it in 1967". (www.internetsociety.org, 2010) The ARPANET eventually paved the way for the invention of the internet. The World Wide Web or www which facilitated the proliferation of websites was created by the Conseil Européen pour la Recherche

Nucléaire, or European Council for Nuclear Research (CERN), a provisional body founded in 1952 with the mandate of establishing a world-class fundamental physics research organization in Europe". The first ever website belonged to CERN and was created in 1993. (home.web. cern.ch, 2015)

The next round of new media development brought in the concept of the email. Electronic mail completely revolutionized the way people communicated as letters, attached documents could be sent immediately and the delivery of the same was also ascertained. Some studies say that the "email is much older than ARPANet or the Internet. It was never invented; it evolved from very simple beginnings.

With the World Wide Web, email started to be made available with friendly web interfaces by providers such as Yahoo and Hotmail. Usually this was without charge. Now that email was affordable, everyone wanted at least one email address, and the medium was adopted by not just millions, but hundreds of millions of people." (Peter I, The history of email, www.nethistory.info, 2011)

The next generation of new media tools are better known as the social media, which facilitates inter personal as well commercial communication on a real time basis through the world wide web. Facebook and Orkut started operations in 2004 giving millions of users an opportunity to share their views, photographs, videos etc with the rest of the world. While Google's product Orkut wound up operations in 2014, many other social media platforms have redefined the definition of communication.

While Facebook facilitates the sharing of views, photographs, web links, videos etc among friends, Twitter has brought in the concept of microblogging where the users have to confine their views and opinions to only 280 characters. Interestingly, its short format has encouraged many celebrities, politicians etc to take to Twitter since conveying a short message and reaching out to millions of 'followers' is neither time consuming nor expensive. The effective use of social media by the Bharatiya Janata Party as a public relations tool was one of the main reasons for the party's resounding victory in the Lok Sabha elections in 2014. The same formula was repeated with greater success in the elections of 2019 as well.

With the passage of time, the social media space has further evolved. Apart from Facebook and Twitter there are many more products of the same nature. Google's Youtube is a video sharing platform. The popularity of Youtube has reached such a stage that no Hollywood or Indian film is ever released without first sharing the trailer on this platform. Instagram is a photosharing platform, which is also gaining popularity rapidly. Similarly, Linkdin is another very popular social media site for professionals. Now it has almost become imperative in the corporate world to check a prospective employee's Linkdin profile before proceeding with the recruitment process.

Skype is a telecommunications application software product that specializes in providing video chat and voice calls from computers, tablets, and mobile devices via the Internet to other devices or telephones/smart phones. Though launched back in 2003, off late this software has gained great popularity. Zoom, which facilitates video conferencing from the confines of one's home gained tremendous popularity during the prolonged lockdowns that the world witnessed due to the Covid 19 pandemic in 2020. Important official meetings, online classes for students, reunion of friends, product launches took place via Zoom. The same trend continues even now.

Google Plus, the social media product of the Google stable could not gain the kind of popularity that other Google products have gained and was shut down in 2019. Snapchat, a multimedia messaging app, was the first application to focus on mobile based usage. It also pioneered the concept of uploading 'stories' where photos and videos would remain visible for 24 hours and then would become inaccessible.

TikTok, a China based video messaging app, launched in 2016 had also become immensely successful. Its largest market was in India, where the app was used extensively by the rural and semi urban population. The app is today available in 40 languages across the world. It was, however, banned in India in June, 2020. Tinder, a dating app is rewriting the rules of socialisation and has gained great popularity among the younger generation.

Similarly, there are hundreds of other social media sites dealing with a range of topics such as music, video sharing, photography, marketing, microblogging, dating, professional enhancement etc. Market leader Facebook was the first social network to surpass 1 billion registered accounts and currently sits at almost 2.45 billion monthly active users. Sixth-ranked photo-sharing app Instagram had 1 billion monthly active accounts. (Clement, J. www.statista.com, 2020)

Interestingly, apart from the above mentioned primarily English language applications, there are many sites with considerable presence in specific regions. Vkontakte is a popular social media site with presence in Russia, Ukraine and to a lesser extent Kazakhstan, Moldova, Belarus and Israel. Similarly Badoo is popular in countries like Italy, Spain, France and parts of Latin America. (www.monitor. icef.com, 2012)

China does not allow globally used social media platforms such as Facebook on its soil. As a result, an ecosystem of internally developed social media channels has become popular in China. Aided by a huge population and a massive geographical area, these social media applications are among the most popular worldwide in terms of number of users. Sina Weibo, a microblogging site, developed on the lines of Twitter has over 300 million users and is among the most popular social media sites in China. Renren, Douban and Qzone are the other social media platforms catering to a large population in China.

The user profiles of all these platforms are remarkably different from each other. Depending on the target audience, Public Relations professionals all over the world now look at these sites as potential carriers of their message. These are platforms where they can reach their desired customer base directly without any via media.

Social networking in the regional languages has become very popular in India also with many people using Hindi, Bengali and other languages in their scripts for expressing opinions on the site. This way, these sites have moved beyond the domain of the English speaking elite of the nation.

In addition, many Indian start-ups have come up with social media platforms which are available in Indian languages. Vokal, a Bengaluru based vernacular social media platform has been rolled out in 10 Indian languages. The platform, works like, Quora, the Q&A platform, where people can ask questions and get them answered by fellow users. Another platform, Share Chat is available in 14 Indian languages. Share Chat is a content sharing platform where people can share content – photos, videos or written content in vernacular languages.

"India is expected to see strong growth in social media and content users in next few years, with 200 million more users expected to be added till 2022, according to RedSeer Consulting. Currently, this market has a duopoly — Google and Facebook. The digital advertising market at the end of last year was pegged at $3 billion, according to RedSeer Consulting." (Venkatesh, G. 2019)

Share Chat, offering services in multiple languages

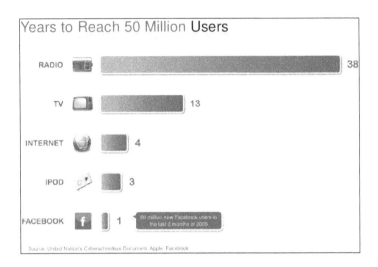

The United Nations Cyberschoolbus, a forum designed to educate and raise awareness about the United Nations among students interested in model UN sessions or related research projects, had done a study on the time that a medium takes to reach 50 million users with a message. In this study, it was found that while radio took 38 years to reach 50 million users, television took 13 years to reach that many people, social media site Facebook took only one year to reach the same number of people.

"Social media has become an ingrained part of our everyday lives. It's one of the main ways we communicate with one another. To put it into perspective, the total worldwide population is currently 7.7 billion. Within that, there are 3.499 billion active social media users." (**www.addthis.com**, 2019)

Blogs, which initially seemed like platforms for the expression of one's creative instincts today is an industry in itself. All sectors have their dedicated blogs and the bloggers are often invited for briefings and requested to write about specific products and services by the promoters of those products or services. Bloggers meets are a common phenomenon which are used by public relations professionals to get their information across to the target users.

Other new age innovations such as search engine optimization and geo targeting are also integral parts of new media. Through search engine optimization, efforts are made to reach out to the readers by using key words in the web content which would help the content in featuring prominently on the list generated by the search engines. In geo targeting, data about the location of the user is collected and relevant information is sent across in the form of advertisements or 'suggestions' in case of social media.

Another comparatively recent facet of new media is the increasing popularity of web based messaging services. WhatsApp with a user base of about 1.5 billion subscribers world over (www.statista.com, 2018) is leading the sector while many other players in the market are also vying for attention such as Line and Wechat. These messaging services have also gained immense popularity since heavy videos, audios can also be seamlessly sent along with pictures. From the commercial perspective, groups can be created with a large number of users as a result of which, a large number of people can be conveyed a message at one go. The difference with the SMS services of the mobile service operators is that in case of these web based applications, audio visual data can be seamlessly sent.

This sector is also witnessing very rapid growth and development. 'Telegram', a US based app, which started its journey in 2013, claims to be the fastest messaging app in the industry. It can accommodate groups of up to 200,000 people in one group unlike Whatsapp or other such apps. This feature helps for commercial activities as a large number of people can be covered at one go.

All these innovations have been made possible because of the the advent of the smart phones. These smart phones not only provide the routine calling services, but have excellent internet surfing features as a result of which social media as well as ecommerce sites can easily be accessed through these mobile handsets. Operating systems such as Andriod, Blackberry, Apple and Windows facilitate the surfing of a range of sites as well as applications keeping the user connected round the clock to the rest of the world.

In the 1990s, the Personal Digital Assistant (PDA) sets gained popularity which ran on operating systems made by brands like Palm, Blackberry and Windows. In 1996, Nokia released the Nokia 9000 Communicator which combined a PDA based on the GEOS V3.0 operating system from Geoworks with a digital cellular phone based on the Nokia 2110, which is often regarded as one of the primary versions of the smart phone.

In 2007, Apple Inc. introduced the iPhone, one of the first smartphones to use a multi-touch interface. The iPhone was notable for its use of a large touchscreen for direct finger input as its main means of interaction, instead of a stylus, keyboard, or keypad typical for smartphones at the time. (www.engadget.com, 2007)

2008 saw the release of the first phone to use Android called the HTC Dream (also known as the T-Mobile G1). Android is an open-source platform founded by Andy Rubin and now owned by Google. Although Android's adoption was relatively slow at first, it started to gain widespread popularity in 2010, and now dominates the market.

These new platforms led to the decline of earlier ones. Microsoft, for instance, started a new OS from scratch, called Windows Phone. Nokia abandoned Symbian and partnered with MS to use Windows Phone on its smartphones. Windows Phone then became the third-most-popular OS. Palm's webOS was bought by Hewlett-Packard and later sold to LG Electronics for use on LG smart TVs. BlackBerry Limited, formerly known as Research In Motion, also made a new platform from scratch, BlackBerry 10.

Almost simultaneously, the computer market was also undergoing tremendous evolution. The traditional personal computer was being gradually replaced by laptops, which were lighter, sleeker and could be carried anywhere. Now tablets have taken over the space of the laptops. These are small audio visual wonders which can be used for almost all the services the laptop offers. In addition, many tablets also offer calling services which is an added bonus. While the laptop would have a screen of about 14 to 15 inches, the tablet is just half the size and can effortlessly sneak into pockets. The market is of course plush with such products of varied sizes which have different configurations but more or less perform similar tasks.

Smart phones and tablets ensured that using the new media tools was not confined indoors. Now people could access these tools on the move, which led to a very fast increase in the number of users. In fact, now the number of mobile internet users would easily outnumber those using the internet from a personal computer or a laptop. It is indeed interesting that devices such as tablets were seen as mere fantasies even in the fifties and the sixties of the last century. In the 1968 film, 2001: A Space Odyssey, the reference of a 'newspad' can be seen, which is very similar to the modern day tablet.

Apple's IPad was launched in the year 2010, and it gave the tablet market a real fillip. Subsequently, almost all other computer as well as mobile brands entered the fray and today the tablet market world over has become extremely competitive as well as price sensitive.

"The first recognisable apps came with Psion's range of handheld computers – mostly PDAs – that used the EPOC operating system. First released in the early 90s the sixteen bit machines (SIBO) which ran EPOC allowed users programmes such as a word processor, database, spreadsheet and diary. Later models in the range, running a 32-bit OS, would come with up to 2MB RAM and allow users to add additional apps via software packs (or via download if you were lucky enough to own a modem). EPOC, which was programmed in OPL (Open Programming Language) and allowed users to create their own apps, would later form the backbone of the Symbian operating system." (Bates S., A History of Mobile Application Development, 2014)

Because of the rapid proliferation of mobile devices, the growth of mobile applications has also gained popularity. Generally, referred to as 'apps' these are custom made platforms which can be accessed directly on the mobile or tablet without accessing the internet. Detailed information can be taken from the app even when it is offline, therefore, reducing the requirement to access the internet all the time. This facility has particularly become popular among the ecommerce companies since they can conveniently load all details in the app, and once downloaded the user can keep surfing even when he is offline. Popular ecommerce based clothing line Myntra had experimented with its business strategy by shifting to an entirely app based business model, which probably indicates towards the future when app based systems will rule the new media world.

It is probably impossible to present an absolutely updated account of the world of new media because, by the time this publication would come out, the sector will have evolved further. However, it would be safe to say that whatever innovations and improvements take place in this sector, they shall be internet based and the smart phones along with the army of laptops and tablets will be the main platforms for carrying out activities using the new media tools.

Chapter 3

New Media as a Tool of Public Relations

As new media tools started gaining popularity, it was apparent that they were going to completely change the way mainstream media worked. Now, everyone had the power to write, the freedom to express. The exalted position of journalists and the mainstream media as the gatekeeper of information now ceased to exist anymore. Now celebrities, corporate houses, political parties could all maintain their own Facebook or Twitter accounts and interact with the world. They could convey what they wanted and even dispute or criticize any reportage done by the mainstream media.

In such a scenario, the sphere of public relations was also bound to change. Its skill sets now not only needed smart communicators who could interact and pitch stories in the media apart from communicating effectively with key stakeholders, now public relations professionals were also required to know the knowhow of using new media.

Now, let us analyze how new media tools are employed in public relations and what are their benefits in comparison to the traditional communication tools which have been in existence for many years now.

Benefits

Low cost campaigns

With the passage of time, the cost of advertising through the print as well as electronic media has tremendously increased. For maximum visibility, it has become imperative to target only the publications with the highest circulation or the channels with the best Television Rating Points (TRP) and for obvious reasons, buying space in such premium media is very expensive.

For example, the rate of a display advertisement on the Delhi edition of The Times of India per square centimetre would cost over a whopping Four Thousand Rupees (www.timesofindia.releasemyad.com). Similarly, even as per the discounted rates of the Directorate of Audio Visual Publicity (DAVP), the per 10 seconds rate of leading entertainment channel Star Plus for the prime time 8 to 11 PM slot is over Fifty Thousand Rupees (www.davp.nic.in). Despite the huge expenditure, the statistical data available about the 'reach' of the campaigns is inaccurate and vague.

In contrast, opening pages on social media sites like Facebook and Twitter cost absolutely nothing. Anybody with decent knowledge of computers can start a social media page. Even if any organization chooses to employ a professional agency for the purpose, the whole exercise wouldn't be as expensive as the print and electronic media advertisements.

However, it must be added that the algorithms which decide how much reach a certain post gets, have become complicated in almost all social media platforms. If anyone wants to reach out to a large audience, then he or she will have to mandatorily buy 'likes' or 'followers'. All social media channels have realized the immense business potential that their products have. As a result, it has become more difficult to reach out to a large audience organically. Having said that, we can still conclude that overall, this new medium is still much cheaper than the conventional tools which have been traditionally in use.

Similarly, for starting websites with only basic information, the cost is negligible. There are many domain space providers who provide dot.com addresses without any expenditure. There are many small time entrepreneurs all over the world who have made it big after starting to promote their products or services through humble websites. In India, the e-commerce site, Flipkart had made a very humble beginning as a site selling books. Today it is a multi-million dollar behemoth selling almost everything. Such has been its success, that in 2018, US based retail giant Walmart purchased a majority stake in the company.

Immediate Feedback

The exorbitant cost of reaching out to customers through the newspapers as well as television channels has been discussed earlier. However, the extent of their reach or the supposed success or failure of the campaign is very difficult to assess. Campaign planners often rely on TRP reports or circulation data issued by the Audit Bureau of Circulation (ABC) for selecting media but there is practically no reliable way to find out whether enough number of readers or viewers have read or seen the intended message.

In case of social media, however, the exact data about the people who have seen the message can be easily found out. The first look of the film 'Zero' was viewed by over 17 million people on Youtube within three months of its uploading which would have given its producers sufficient idea that the first look of the film had been liked by the people.

The websites, blogs can also leave message boards below the desired information where the readers can post their comments after reading the information. This is almost akin to the 'Letters to the Editor' column of newspapers. The only difference is that, in case of the websites, blogs, social media pages etc, the feedback is immediate.

Control over the dissemination of information

For ages now, public relations professionals all over the world have issued press releases or organized press conferences to share their information or opinion. However, as mentioned earlier, in such cases, the 'gatekeeper' of the information is the journalist. There are innumerable cases, where the journalists do not present an information or opinion in the manner in which the concerned organization wants them to. There are instances, when the press releases are not carried at all leaving the public relations professionals with very few options, since carrying the information in a certain manner as desired by the concerned organization is not binding on the journalists and they are absolutely free to add their own perspective to it.

With the advent of the internet – the websites and the social media, the public relations professionals need not rely on the journalists for sharing their information with the rest of the world. In the changed scenario, they are themselves the 'gatekeeper' of the information and can reach millions of readers even without relying on the conventional media. Increasingly, many politicians, film stars, sportspersons are writing their own blogs and tweeting the information about their activities to the readers directly.

The Twitter handle of the Prime Minister's office has a whopping 33.9 million followers (www.twitter.com). Therefore, if any information is shared on this handle, it would reach a huge number of people immediately. Similarly, the websites also have provisions by which the number of visitors to the site can be calculated. This gives an accurate idea about the number of people who have visited the site.

Instant reach

Another major advantage of the internet based media tools is that the reach of the information is absolutely immediate. Once any piece of information is put on social media or on a website, it immediately reaches every corner of the world wherever the internet is available. In case of conventional media especially newspapers, television or the radio, the immediacy is absent as they would share the information desired only at their specified time. In addition, newspapers, television or radio channels do not have the capacity to reach every corner of the world without relying on the internet.

New media penetration in India

One of the long standing arguments against the increasing use of new media tools in India in either PR or advertising is the supposedly low penetration of internet based platforms among the population, especially in the rural areas and among senior citizens and women. "With over 560 million internet users, India is the second largest online market in the world, ranked only behind China. By 2021, there will be over 600 million internet users in India. Despite the large base of internet users, only 34 percent of the Indian population could access the internet in 2017. Even then, this was a big increase when compared to the previous few years, when the internet penetration rate stood at approximately a little over 10 percent. At the same time, almost 70 percent of the internet users in the country were noted to be men, compared to just 30 percent of female internet users.

Roughly 29 percent of the country's population, that is around 230 million people accessed the internet via their mobile phones in 2018. This was a large majority of the overall digital population in the south Asian country. However Mobile internet usage and access varies on certain socio-economic conditions including urban and rural regions in the country. As of 2016, India had an estimated 262 million mobile internet users living in urban communities, and 109 million living in rural areas.

One aspect wherein India shares the characteristics of other global internet users is its passion for social media. It was estimated that by 2023, there would be around 448 million social network users in India. A significant increase from 2018, when this figure stood at about 326 million. Furthermore the share of Indian population that access social networks is expected to jump from 22 percent in 2017 to over 26 percent in 2019. Amongst all of the social media available, YouTube and Facebook were the most popular social networking sites. In fact, with 281 million Facebook users in the country in 2018, India had the largest Facebook user base in the world. WhatsApp, Instagram and Facebook Messenger were some of the other popular social networking sites in the country." (www. statista.com, 2020)

India's immense internet potential had been recognized many years back. The India@digital.bharat report compiled in January, 2015 by the Boston Consulting Group (BCG) and the Internet and Mobile Association of India (IAMAI) had claimed that India would topple the United States as the second largest internet using nation by the year 2018. The Mary Meeker's Internet Trends Report 2019, informed that India had become the second largest internet user base in the world with 12 percent of the world's internet users behind China which had 21 percent of the world's internet users. The United States was the third with eight percent of the world's internet users..

The India@digital.bharat report had also found that India had already emerged as one of the top markets globally for social media as well as e-commerce sites. "India is the second largest market for social networking giants such as Facebook and LinkedIn. 58,000 new users get connected on to a social network every day. E-commerce is shifting users from shopping in stores to shopping on the go. Chinese smartphone manufacturer Xiaomi recently sold 75,000 of its Mi3 models exclusively online in five rounds of flash sales on Flipkart, with most of the sales lasting for less than 10 seconds." (www.iamwire.com, 2015)

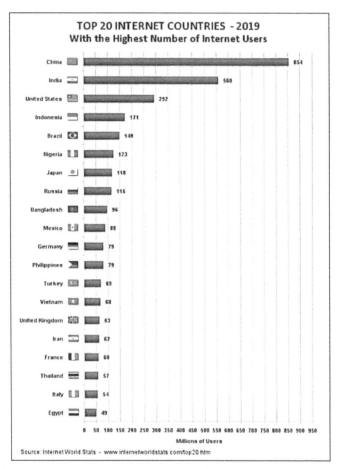

(www.internetworldstats.com, 2019)

On the basis of the studies mentioned above, it is obvious that internet based media has great potential in the country. With its massive population and vast territory, internet is the most potent tool to reach the maximum number of people in the shortest possible time. While in terms of percentage, the penetration still seems less, it is sure to expand exponentially in the years to come.

Urban India with an estimated population of 455 million already has 295 million using the internet. Rural India, with an estimated population of 918 million as per 2011 census, has only 186 million internet users leaving out potential 732 million users in rural India. Internet penetration in Urban India was 64.84% in December 2017 as compared to 60.6% last December. In comparison, rural Internet penetration has grown from 18% last December to 20.26% in December 2017. (www.economictimes.com, 2018)

Some Early New Media Case Studies

While the internet started holding sway over various aspects of our lives right from the start of the new millennium, it was only by the mid of 2000s that new media started having a distinct role in public relations. Ever since, there have been many new media success stories world over where, PR campaigns run on the internet based platforms have made a huge impact. Let us have a look at some of those case studies of early successes in the domain of new media usage. We shall study a few more case studies in greater details in the subsequent chapters.

US Presidential Elections, 2008

One of the earliest examples of effective use of new media as a public relations tool was the the 2008 US presidential campaign of the eventual winner Barack Obama. The Democratic candidate used Twitter and Facebook to differentiate his campaign. The social media pages were constantly updated and a lot of focus was laid on continuous interaction with the followers. The effective use of the social networking sites gave Obama's campaign access to e-mail addresses, as posted on social network profile pages. With such an exhaustive email database, a separate email based campaign was also launched.

Lok Sabha Elections, 2014

Not many years later, present Indian Prime Minister, Narendra Modi repeated the same new media strategy with great success in the 2014 general elections, in which party, the Bharatiya Janata Party (BJP) thumped to a massive victory. With the hash tag #Achchedin (good days), Modi launched a multipronged campaign on social media sites such as Facebook and Twitter. The party's publicity videos were launched via youtube and no stone was left unturned to turn the videos viral. Maximum attempts were also made to gauge the mood of the voters. The campaign was managed very professionally by a specialized agency.

"Just like Obama became popular as the first social media president of U.S.A, Modi, popularly known as NaMo, also notched the tag of first social media prime minister of India. Talking about facts and statistics, Narendra Modi also became the second most-liked politician on Facebook. Modi's achievements, credentials and impeccable personality are not the only reason behind this popularity on social media. His party impressively stormed social media platforms by engaging the users into important conversations. The tagline "Ab Ki Bar Modi Sarkar" and "Twinkle Twinkle Little Star Ab Ki Baar Modi Sarkar" became viral on Facebook, Twitter, and Instagram, and left a lingering message in the minds of people. The volunteers of the party struck conversations with common people and understood their frame of mind and attitude, which in turn helped them to create a buzz.

Where on one side politicians were trying to form a direct connection with the potential voters on Facebook and Twitter by posting and tweeting regularly, the active users on the other hand began to engage with each other on the political front. Social media was not only a way for our netas to make a difference, but it also gave a chance to people to comprehend each other's mind-set and influence opinions by sharing knowledge and spreading awareness on a personal level. Indian politicians clearly followed the footsteps of Obama and discreetly used the hashtag strategy on Twitter. Trending hastags like #Election2014, #NaMo, and #ArvindKejriwal made people aware about the latest elections developments." (http://centerac.com, 2014)

The Ice Bucket Challenge, 2014

The Ice Bucket Challenge was started as a campaign to raise funds for the treatment and research of the Amyotrophic Lateral Sclerosis, popularly known as the ALS disease. The campaign went viral on social media and many celebrities all over the world participated in it. In 2014, the campaign collected over a hundred million US dollars.

"It was a really viral campaign which had the participation of several celebrities (including Mark Zuckerberg, the CEO of Facebook, the social network where this action went more viral than anywhere else), bloggers, and a lot of social network users who spontaneously participated in this action." (www.augure.com, 2014)

Oreo Biscuits Social Media Campaign, 2013

Global biscuit brand Oreo was one of the first brands in this sector to effectively use the new media tools. Their social media campaigns, at one stage had made them one of the fastest growing brands on Facebook globally.

"Oreo India had launched a Facebook-led social media campaign which made them one of the fastest growing Facebook pages in the world at that time. The brand created content units which connected it with an important event of the day on which the post was made.

For example, on June 21, it posted a visual update reminding people that it was the longest day of the year, an obvious fact. But to connect it with the brand, it used a stretched pack of Oreo biscuits. The first thing you notice about the posts is the use of the product and its packaging as a visual device to explain the event that it talks about in the post. Later on, Oreo India also took its 'Daily dunks' initiative to the community by launching Dunkathon. It had done a wonderful job with their innovative content creation." (www.socialsamosa.com, 2013)

Parle G's New Media Campaign, 2013

Popular biscuit maker Parle G was looking to start an online activity which would reemphasize the brand's philosophy that children get energy and become more attentive in their daily activities if they eat the biscuit. Therefore, they launched the 'Parle G Future Genius' campaign with the help of a microsite.

"Parle G was attempting to reach out to parents and kids by engaging them in an online activity to reinstate the brand philosophy. The campaign was an opportunity to interact with the core target group and build a strong relationship with them.

They had launched a microsite thefuturegenius.com and roped in Ruskin Bond, a famous writer for the site. The micro site contains a couple of sections namely Genius Gyaan, Parents Quotient and Diary of a Genius.

In a nutshell, the campaign clearly demonstrated that it is not just content that works, it is content, which adds value to the society that does the magic." (www.socialsamosa. com, 2013)

The Dunk That Junk Campaign, 2016

MTV India carried out the #DunkThatJunk campaign in 2016 with great success. Almost on the lines of the 'Swachh Bharat Abhiyan' of the Government of India, the campaign intended to promote the cause of hygiene and cleanliness. Many celebrities from the film world including superstar Shahrukh Khan were roped in to extend support to the campaign.

"Attempting to bring about a transformation in the mentality from the root, MTV through their campaign #DunkThatJunk raised the issue of cleanliness." (www. socialsamosa.com, 2016)

As part of the Junkyard Project, MTV India invited people to post videos on the social media site Twitter while junking some waste in the dustbin. It also said that for every 10 such videos one dustbin would be installed by MTV. The hashtag #DunkThatJunk became very popular and many celebrities came forward to participate.

Change the Question campaign, 2017

Female clothing and apparel brand Biba's #changethequestion campaign also received rave reviews. The campaign was aimed at stopping the practice of body shaming women on the basis of their body size or figure. A minute long film was released on YouTube which showed how a family of three beautifully dealt with the issue of body shaming.

The video went viral on Facebook and Twitter and was an instant hit especially among the women. A #changethequestion contest was also conducted where prizes were given away to women participants on answering some questions.

In conclusion, we may say that, new media has become extremely popular as a tool of communication for its many obvious benefits. Cost effectiveness, instant reach and control over the messaging are benefits which have made the domain of communication much easier. We can also sum up that, new media tools suit all kinds of requirements irrespective of the allocated budget, target audience, nature of product etc. Campaigns can be custom designed easily according to requirement of the client. However, it must also be added that the new media world is extremely dynamic and it is continuously evolving. Over the last few years, along with the rapid increase in its usage some very obvious pitfalls have also come into notice. We shall discuss about them in the subsequent chapters.

Chapter 4

New Media and the Indian Public Sector

When it comes to the adoption of the latest technologies available to the public relations professionals, the public sector was initially found to be lagging far behind their private sector counterparts. New media tools such as the internet; its constituents like e-mail services, blogs, podcasts and much later social media were immediately picked by the private sector to take their products and services to the people. However, the government run agencies were rather sluggish to do the same. Most of the government agencies designed their own websites and entities such as the National Informatics Centre (NIC) were created to facilitate the same. But, most of the sites initially proved to be slow, unattractive and in many instances loaded with inaccurate or stale information.

Today, the public relations scenario is becoming more and more interactive. Public relations practitioners are not depending on traditional media tools such as newspapers or television only to air their information. Rather, they are effectively using the social media to launch and promote their products or service. Today, no product starting from a soap to a car would be launched without registering presence in the social media sites such as Facebook or Twitter. The biggest benefit of using the social media is that the product gets immediate feedback from lakhs of people and the whole exercise is not very cost intensive either.

The advent of the new media tools have provided an excellent platform to the market to showcase their products and services. The tools are also interactive with the provision of immediate feedback. Gone are the days when taking out expensive advertisements in newspapers or television channels were the only tool of reaching out to the target audience. Now, companies simply launch low cost social media campaigns and manage to reach thousands of prospective buyers.

Rather unfortunately, the Indian public sector was slow in adapting to these new age innovations. For example, the online reservation service run by the Indian Railways Catering and Tourism Corporation (IRCTC), an undertaking of the Indian Railways was extremely inefficient and often caused inconvenience to the users who depended on it for their travel bookings. As a result, apart from the railway bookings, IRCTC also found it difficult to compete with other private entities such as Thomas Cook, DPauls etc in selling general holiday packages to tourists. However, it would be pertinent to add that post 2016, the ticketing mechanism of IRCTC has shown vast improvement.

Even today, many of these organizations also do not have official Facebook pages or twitter handles, which have become the norm for most of the organizations of the private sector. In many cases, even if they have presence on social media, the same is not properly managed. Therefore, we often notice that whenever, the government run establishments are pitted against the private players in an open market situation, they are found wanting in terms of customer service, which in turn harms their business prospects.

Due to reasons such as procedural delays, red tape and on occasions, plain reluctance to adopt something new, the public sector fails to effectively use these measures. For example, the state owned Bharat Sanchar Nigam Limited (BSNL), the Mahanagar Telephone Nigam Limited (MTNL) are running in losses in comparison to the burgeoning business of corporate entities like Reliance Jio. While it cannot be denied that the BSNL or the MTNL have also failed to provide quality services, but at the same time, they have also failed to sell their products as efficiently as their private sector rivals.

In the banking sector also, the private banks such as HDFC and ICICI have introduced a slew of new age services based on new media. "Banks like ICICI Bank Ltd., HDFC Bank Ltd. etc. are thus looking to position themselves as one stop financial shops. These banks have tied up with computer training companies, computer manufacturers, Internet Services Providers and portals for expanding their Net banking services, and widening their customer base." (Report on Internet Banking, RBI, 2001).

The above mentioned report shows that private banks were using new media effectively even more than a decade back, while their public sector counterparts with much larger market shares in the banking sector were slow to adapt to the same. Probably, many more such examples can be shown in the other sectors as well.

The situation of the public sector undertakings in the states is even more discouraging. Though they also have to compete with the private sector in many spheres, their public relations infrastructure is mostly archaic and old fashioned. Most states have a directorate of information and publicity which still carries out age old functions such as publishing government advertisements, print publicity folders etc. But there is hardly any effort to reach out to the people through the more modern means. Though, it may be added that many chief ministers and senior ministers have professionally managed Facebook and Twitter accounts through which they communicate with the people.

For example, road transport is one sector in which most state governments operate and compete with their private rivals. But barring a few state transport corporations, none of the other such undertakings have any web presence. Transport corporations of states like Rajasthan and Himachal Pradesh, which are popular with tourists, have pretty effective websites with provisions such as web booking of tickets. They also have presence on the social media. But similar corporations from many other states have no such facility.

On the contrary, private bus operators have been utilising the web for business even in the interior areas of states like Assam. Jagannath Travels, a private operator which runs buses between the state's nerve centre Guwahati and the southern Assam towns of Silchar, Karimganj and Hailakandi started offering tickets on the popular bus ticketing site www.redbus.in back in 2014, which gave them a definite business advantage over the state run Assam State Transport Corporation (ASTC) which has started booking through Redbus only recently. Many people travel up to Guwahati by air or railway and want to immediately travel to these towns by connecting buses. Such passengers want to pre book tickets for the buses as getting tickets real time is often very difficult. ASTC has also launched a ticketing website apart from revamping its corporate website, but all these developments have come quite late in comparison to the private sector counterparts.

However, with the ever increasing penetration of the internet, the communication strategies of the public sector are also gradually turning their attention towards the new media tools. The National Democratic Alliance government led by Narendra Modi which came to power in 2014, has put a lot of focus on new media as an important part of their communication strategy.

The government today runs a number of schemes aimed towards introducing more and more internet supported services which automatically decrease the possibilities of corruption and red tape. The National e-governance plan was one of those ambitious projects launched in 2006 to take the basic facilities provided by the government to the people more conveniently.

"The National e-Governance Plan (NeGP) has been formulated by the Department of Electronics and Information Technology (DEITY) and Department of Administrative Reforms and Public Grievances (DARPG). The Union Government approved the NeGP, comprising of 27 Mission Mode Projects (MMPs) and 10 components on May 18, 2006.

The NeGP aims at improving delivery of Government services to citizens and businesses with the following vision:

Make all Government services accessible to the common man in his locality, through common service delivery outlets and ensure efficiency, transparency & reliability of such services at affordable costs to realize the basic needs of the common man." (www.india.gov.in, 2015)

E-tendering has also been introduced in all public sector undertakings and government departments. The government is gradually proceeding towards enforcing e-tendering for all high value tenders. Many state governments have introduced 'time bound services' mechanisms as per which the basic public services such as issue of birth/ death certificates, pension payments etc are to be made within a specific period of time. For such assignments as well, internet based services are being employed. In such cases, the internet based facilities are playing a major role in also eliminating corruption and remove red tape from the system.

Other public interface media of the government such as the public grievances mechanisms and the applications received under the Right to Information Act, 2005 are also being made available online by the central government as well as many state governments. Transactions in public sector banks, post offices, bill payment facilities of water, power, telecom utilities are also turning online bringing people relief from the perennial problems such as queuing up at the counters or taking leave from the offices for completing such assignments.

In the field of transport also, the internet based platforms created by the government are playing a major role and have shown improvement in terms of speed of delivery and quality of service.. The advance railway reservation system maintained by the Indian Railway Catering and Tourism Corporation (IRCTC) books on average four to five lakh tickets every day. The government run carrier, Air India also has e-ticketing services, which have provided great relief to the passengers. Their presence on the social media platforms are also professionally managed and regularly updated.

The Digital India Campaign

The central government, in July 2015, has launched the 'Digital India' campaign which aims at providing the basic services to the citizens through the information technology enabled platforms and also enhance the use of such platforms for official functioning to eliminate age old lacunae connected to government functioning such as red tape, corruption, too much paper work etc.

The 'Digital India' programme has three broad visions - Infrastructure as a Utility to Every Citizen, Governance & Services on Demand and Digital Empowerment of Citizens. The programme has identified nine 'pillars' on which its activities will be based. These are - broadband highways, e-governance, electronics manufacturing, universal access to phones, e-kranti (electronic delivery of services), IT for jobs, public internet access programme, information for all, early harvest programmes.

The programme has many ambitious targets such as taking broadband connectivity to over 2,50,000 village panchayats, online public grievance redressal, workflow automation, e-education, e-healthcare, automation in judicial procedures, job creation etc. the programme intends to spend about a hundred thousand crores on the implementation of the existing schemes and another 13,000 crores for new schemes. Many existing digital media related schemes have also been incorporated into the umbrella programme called 'Digital India'. (Digital India document, 2015)

"Government of India launched National e-Governance Plan (NeGP) in 2006. 31 Mission Mode Projects covering various domains were initiated. Despite the successful implementation of many e-Governance projects across the country, e-Governance as a whole has not been able to make the desired impact and fulfil all its objectives.

It has been felt that a lot more thrust is required to ensure e-Governance in the country promote inclusive growth that covers electronic services, products, devices and job opportunities. Moreover, electronic manufacturing in the country needs to be strengthened.

In order to transform the entire ecosystem of public services through the use of information technology, the Government of India has launched the Digital India programme with the vision to transform India into a digitally empowered society and knowledge economy." (www.digitalindia.gov.in, 2015)

The above mentioned campaign is an ambitious initiative taken by the Government of India and if implemented successfully, will bring in much awaited reforms and improvement in the government service delivery mechanism in the Indian public sector which suffers from perennial challenges such as rampant corruption, inefficiency and lack of accountability.

However, despite the challenges, the Prime Minister's office seems to be leading by example. The PMO is using new media very effectively as a public relations medium and reaching out to millions of people every day. The Twitter and Facebook accounts of the Prime Minister share photographs of the activities of his office every day and the response of the followers is also huge depicting the success and popularity of the initiative.

While the Facebook page of the Prime Minister's office has a whopping 13 million 'likes', the Twitter handle has over 34 million followers and has already sent over 25,000 Tweets so far (as on 21st April, 2020). The Prime Minister uses these platforms to convey a lot of his vision, ideas and opinions on a range of issues. Social media users also tag the Twitter handle regarding a lot of issues facing the country which gives the Prime Minister's office some idea about the mood of the nation on important events as well as issues.

In addition to the general websites of the government of India and specifically the Prime Minister's office, a new website called www.mygov.in was launched in 2014 solely with the purpose of enhancing the engagement of the public with the government. On this website, the visitors can register and then send complaints, grievances, and suggestions on the issues facing the country. As on 21st April, 2020 the website had over ten million registered members. The website had over seven lakh submissions and over 42 lakh comments, which clearly indicates its massive reach.

The Prime Minister is also using social media very effectively by encouraging people to participate in various campaigns and post on a range of topics with specific hash tags. This helps the Prime Minister to gauge the popularity of his schemes and polices and also raises awareness about a range of socially relevant issues.

For example, in June, 2015, the Prime Minister, Mr. Narendra Modi stressed on the importance of education and opportunities for the girl children and encouraged fathers to post their photographs with their daughters with the hash tag #SelfieWithDaughter, during his monthly radio address called 'Mann ki baat'. The campaign, inspired by a similar campaign launched in a village in Haryana to promote gender equality, has since trended on social media in a major way. The Prime Minister had also promised to retweet the best photographs and messages accompanying them.

The social media campaign has been launched to promote the programme 'Beti Bachao Beti Padhao', which is oriented towards the promotion of the education of the girl children and prevention of the age old menace called female infanticide.

On the lines of the Prime Minister's office, all other ministers of the central government have also started social media accounts for their ministries. For example, the Ministry of Railways also has a dedicated official Facebook page, with more than 1.6 million 'likes'. The page also regularly updates information about the various in initiatives taken by the ministry with photographs and videos.

Public Relations is about communicating effectively with the people and reaching out to them to convey relevant messages and listening to their complaints and suggestions. On these counts, the social media outreach efforts of the Prime Minister are indeed praiseworthy. His tweets and posts are often compiled into news by the mainstream media and whenever any citizen is directly benefitted by communicating on these forums, the same gets tremendous media coverage and increases the goodwill of the government.

To conclude, it may be said, that new media usage in government communication is still evolving and maturing. Today, on the lines of the communication strategies adopted by the Prime Minister, all Government departments, undertakings or autonomous bodies have presence online especially on social media. All ministers, senior bureaucrats, police forces, educational institutions are communicating with their target audiences through social media. However, concerns still remain on the efficacy of these platforms on all sections of the society. Some of the hurdles in this regard are enumerated below.

- **Use of language in social media:** A lot of social media messaging by the government now a days is taking place in the vernacular languages which has helped in taking these messages to all strata of the society. The vernacular languages have also got a new lease of life as more users are increasingly turning towards their native languages leaving English for use on social media. However, despite these improvements, English continues to remain the main language of communication on the internet. Most websites, mobile applications run by the government as well have English as the primary language. In many cases, it has been noticed that the Hindi sites are not as regularly maintained as the English sites. In many states, government sites do not have equally well designed vernacular language site for the people of that state. As the government enages itself in more extensive use of new media in its communication with the masses, this aspect will have to be worked on.

- **Reach and effectiveness of the websites:** While social media platforms such as Facebook, Twitter and especially Whatsapp have made rapid inroads into the rural population of India as well, some government sites which offer details of the many government welfare schemes are still not very popular among the masses. In some cases, the sites are not very attractively designed while in some other instances, even if they have a lot of quality content, they are not promoted among the target audience aggressively. Another perennial problem is the presence of stale information in the sites which also end up misguiding the people. As the internet gradually becomes the new platform through which the government intends to take its welfare measures to the people directly, these issues will have to be tackled at the earliest.

- **Internet penetration:** Another major challenge that the government today confronts is the issue of internet penetration across the length and breadth of the country. In the preceding chapter, we have seen that internet usage in India has increased exponentially in the last few years. In fact, today, India has the second highest number of internet users across the world. Data rates in India are also among the lowest. However, given India's massive population and vast land area, there are still many pockets, especially in the rural belts where internet has not been able to reach. According to a study conducted by CISCO in 2020, India will have a whopping 907 million internet users by 2023. The study also claims that India's internet user base is increasing at a faster rate than its population. However, given India's population of over 1.3 billion, the figure is still less than the total population. In addition, a majority of the internet using population is concentrated in the urban areas. The percentage of internet users among the rural masses would be much lower.

- **Maturity of the target audience:** Internet literacy is a raging issue today. The internet, especially social media has today enabled every single individual with the authority to freely convey his/her ideas and opinions without any editing or filter. The issue of rumours spreading through Whatsapp messages and social media posts has become a major challenge for administrators. Therefore, as the government looks at new media as a potential platform for the dissemination of its welfare policies and as it uses social media to convey details about the work done, it will also have to look into the level of understanding of the target audience. For example, many fake accounts, pages are there on social media which claim to belong to important government departments, functionaries, ministers, prominent leaders etc. They post fake messages regarding new projects, job openings and dupe gullible people. Sometimes, make fake posts regarding government actions such as arrest of a certain individual, or messages with communal overtones are circulated to create unrest among the people. Therefore, internet literacy will have to be made a part of school education, so that all individuals across social or geographical divides develop the maturity to distinguish between genuine and fake messages.

- **Lacunae in grievance redressal:** Another important dimension of using new media as a communication platform is that, a lot of individuals tend to use the new media platforms for grievance redressal. We have seen many examples, of how government departments like the Railways have responded promptly to tweets and facebook posts to help passengers. Former External Affairs Minister, the late Smt. Sushma Swaraj was also very well known for responding to messages from ordinary citizens. The grievance redressal portal of the Government of India is also very helpful in disposing off genuine grievances by people. However, the same can't be said about the grievance redressal mechanisms of all government departments, officials or establishments. As more and more individuals start using internet to know about government policies and actions, they will also try to use the same platforms for airing their grievances and complaints. These also will have to be dealt with great seriousness and commitment.

The scope of new media usage is so profound in governance today that it is extremely difficult to demarcate where new media is being used only as a PR tool and where it is being used as a medium to take policies and facilities directly to the doorstep of the citizen. We may say that if any government initiative reaches the grass-root directly with the help of technology, it also serves as a public relations exercise as the beneficiary would invariably pass on the good word to the people he is acquainted with.

Chapter 5

New Media in the Indian Private Sector

Unlike the public sector, the private sector is generally guided by a much greater requirement of generating profits from its endeavours. They also function in a competitive environment where there are many more players producing similar products or extending similar kind of services. As a result, we often notice that the private sector adapts to new technologies and innovations much faster than the government owned entities. The same also holds good for the use of new media in the domain of public relations in the Indian private sector. The public relations as well as the overall communications strategies of companies have changed significantly with the advent of the new media. For a long time, television and print media advertisements were the corner stones of the public relations as well as advertising strategies of the corporates. However, now new media has occupied that space to a large extent. The use of new media generally has got two dimensions – one is product promotion and the other is grievance redressal. New media tools, especially social media have given the opportunity to handle both these aspects using the same platform. In fact, the other tools of product promotion such as advertising and marketing as a whole can also be easily integrated into the social media platforms without any significant expenditure.

One of the early movers in the Indian private sector as far as the use of new media tools is concerned was Vodafone. In 2009, during the second season of the Indian Premier League, Vodafone started the Zoozoo campaign where white creatures with bloated stomachs were seen promoting the various schemes and products of the telecom major. They made a distinct sound also and were an immediate hit among the customers. However, the campaign designed and executed by Ogilvy and Mather was also unique because they employed the social media in a major way. The Zoozoos had presence on Facebook, Orkut and Twitter. Their videos were also viewed by millions on YouTube. Apart from the official page on Zoozoos which had videos of the campaign apart from contests and other promotional content, many fan based pages also emerged as people really liked the imaginary creatures. In many ways, the Zoozoo campaign set the tone for many more such social media campaigns to follow. The platform of the popular cricket league, IPL was also effectively used by Vodafone to push this campaign.

In the IPL itself, the Kolkata Knight Riders franchise was also among the early movers in the new media domain. They have a dedicated website, a mobile application and a YouTube video blog to reach out to their support base. Today, the KKR franchise has over 16 million followers on Facebook, which is the highest among all the IPL teams. For their supporter engagement campaigns, KKR actively took help of the new media tools right from the beginning of the IPL tournament. The presence of actor Shah Rukh Khan as one of the owners of the franchise was leveraged with his videos. In the initial years, former India captain Sourav Ganguly was also taken as an 'icon player' and he also figured prominently in the promotional campaigns. The same tradition is still being maintained. In 2020,when the IPL was called off because of the Covid 19 pandemic, KKR continued to organize interactions between the players and the fans through its social media channels. In the 'Knights Unplugged' series which aired on Facebook, interactions with prominent players were organized.

Over the last one decade, new media has started to figure very prominently in the communications as well as marketing strategies of the Indian private sector. There is probably no communication campaign that is planned without the use of new media tools. Apart from social media presence, another tool that is being increasingly used is the mobile application. Now for promotion of products and services also, mobile applications are being designed. In addition, prominent mobile applications are used as platforms for major communications and advertising campaigns. For example, the BookMyShow mobile application often has advertisements, contests etc of the films that are slated to release since the app gets huge traffic for booking of movie tickets especially in the urban areas.

Internal communication is another area for which mobile applications are being increasingly used by the major corporate entities. In organizations with huge work forces, internal communication to maintain a coherent team is often as necessary as the external communication strategies. Now-a-days, software firms are also offering custom made solutions to companies for internal communication requirements with the help of mobile applications.

According to a survey done by the Research Firm EY in 2015, almost all the Indian entities surveyed by the firm said that social media was a very integral part of their overall marketing and communications mix. "About 90% of organizations reached out to in this study are planning to spend as much as 15% of their annual marketing budget exclusively on social media, up from 78% organizations in 2013. About 23% respondents stated that their social media budgets were in excess of INR 1million per annum and 14% of the brands spent INR 10-20 million on social media in 2014. There was a decline in the number of brands that spent in excess of INR 20 million from 17.1% in 2013 to 14.3% in 2014 indicating that brands are exceedingly cautious on the returns and are optimizing spends. As integrated campaigns are reckoned as effective, being able to correctly attribute leads, attain conversions and returns to channels, campaigns and devices will determine how budgets are allocated going forward". (www.firstpost.com, 2015)

Mobile applications are also extremely popular and are featuring very prominently in the overall communications mix of the companies across the country. "India is now the world's second largest app market, trailing only China. It has surpassed the US, both in terms of internet users, and app downloads. Explosive growth in India and other emerging markets in Southeast Asia is said to be propelling the global app economy. App analytics provider App Annie, in a recent report, said that India now accounts for nearly 58 billion downloads of the world's 175 billion. In India, app engagement is head and shoulders above mobile browsers. As much as 88 percent of the time spent on mobile was on apps; 12 percent was on mobile browsers. This is in sync with worldwide user behaviour." (www.yourstory.com, 2018)

Another major tool of communication for the Indian corporate sector are the private messaging applications. Whatsapp is a highly popular messaging app, used in India. Owned by Facebook, Whatsapp has around 400 million users in India currently. Other popular messaging applications in use in India are Facebook Messenger, Viber and Telegram. "One of the main reasons that professional messenger communication is seeing such success is simply because messaging apps have enormous reach, globally. WhatsApp is the 3rd most popular social media worldwide, closely following Facebook and Youtube. And unlike Facebook and YouTube, communication over WhatsApp is completely personal and direct. While traditional social media has recently been plagued by privacy concerns, algorithms, and stagnating user numbers, messaging app usage is only growing. It's a force to be reckoned with – and you can see this clearly from social data." (Steup, M. 2018)

"WhatsApp user engagement is high, averaging out the 65 billion messages means users are sending 43 messages per day on average. In addition, with read and receipt indicators WhatsApp users have a lot of psychological pressure to respond to people who are messaging them. Although it's a bit early to know definitively if this effect transfers over to chatting with businesses, there is some evidence to suggest it has." (Kudritskiy, I. 2019)

To tap into this sector, WhatsApp has launched the 'WhatsApp for Business' application. Launched in 2018, the app is absolutely free for download. It has many attractive features for promotion of business such as quick reply, messaging templates etc. it is really helpful for small businesses. Now, a paid version of the app for larger businesses is also available.

"According to Tech Crunch, over 3 million businesses have already taken the leap by using the WhatsApp for Business app. This data is supported by the fact that the app has over 10 million downloads on Google's Play Store. In addition, some have reported that messages have a 99% open rate & 40% + response rate in use cases where WhatsApp for Business is used by universities." (Kudritskiy, I. 2019)

The Indian corporate sector is one of the largest as well as one of the fastest growing markets in the world today. The penetration of the internet is also increasing every day and the worldwide web is reaching newer areas. In such a scenario, the use of new media tools will only continue to increase in the coming days and we will observe many new trends and innovations as well. The entire PR and communications activity will gradually shift its focus on the smart phone away from the print publications and the television. These are indeed exciting times for the Public Relations professionals across the world!!

Chapter 6

Case Studies: Public Sector

To understand the potential of new media as a tool of public relations in the Indian public sector, let us have a look at the case studies of two organizations which have successfully employed these tools as part of their communication strategies. In the subsequent chapters, case studies of such stories in the Indian private sector will also be analysed.

Delhi Traffic Police

The Delhi Traffic Police employs a number of new media options to execute its public relations activities. Traffic management in Delhi is a major challenge as the national capital has more vehicles than all the metropolitan cities of the country. In such a scenario, it becomes absolutely important to communicate the updates on the traffic situation in the city to the motorists on a real time basis and the Delhi Traffic Police employs new media to convey such messages very effectively.

Facebook Page

The Facebook page of the Delhi Traffic Police was introduced in May, 2010 and has since then got more close to three lakh likes. In the description of the page in the 'About' section of the page, Delhi Traffic Police mentions, "Mobility with safety has to be the guiding principle for any Traffic manager. To achieve this, the Traffic unit needs to build its action plan on the four pillars of Education, Regulation, Enforcement and Road Engineering (ERER) – all well known facets of traffic management. The mantra of ERER, however, needs to become a vision shared by all traffic personnel so that they do not remain moribund and freely contribute newer ideas to enhance mobility with safety. Road users, civil society and all other influential individuals and groups - whether governmental, social, religious and political - need to extend their full support to make roads safer." (Facebook.com/delhitrafficpolice, 2010)

The page is maintained on a regular basis with updates about the traffic snarls that take place in the city. On an average, the Facebook page of the Delhi Traffic Police uploads about eight to ten posts a day on the traffic situation in the city. After the solution to the traffic problem in a particular area, the page also posts updates that the snarl has been cleared. In addition, the Facebook page also uploads photographs and videos of the various social service activities taken up by the Police. For examples, photographs of various workshops, seminars etc are also put up on the page.

Facebook pages have the option of reviews, where the visitors can review the quality of a page. On the reviews section, the page has got a rating of 3.2 stars out of five, which indicates that there is scope for further improvement. (as on 29th April, 2020)

Generally, the updates are put up in short and terse language so that the users can easily understand the message. On important occasions, the updates are also put up in Hindi for the users who may not be well conversant with English. For example, a Facebook post reads like this –

"Traffic Alert: Breakdown of DTC bus No. DL 1PC 0626 near AIIMS flyover, in the carriageway from South Extension towards Dhoula Kuan. It is being removed. Inconvenience is regretted.

साउथ एक्सटेंशन से धौला कुआँ की तरफ जाने वाले मार्ग पर AIIMS फ्लाईओवर के पास एक DTC बस No. DL 1PC 0626 ख़राब हो गई है जिसे हटाया जा रहा है | असुविधा के लिए खेद है |"

The idea is obviously to convey the desired information in an easy manner without compromising on any of the relevant details. After the solution to a traffic problem also, the information is shared with the people, **"Traffic Alert: Breakdown HTV near Chirga Delhi removed. Traffic is normal now. चिराग दिल्ली के पास जो HTV खराब हो गया था उसे वहां से हटा दिया गया है | यातायात अब सामान्य है |"**

There is a continuous effort to reply back to the complaints made by the users. Any visitor to the page can post a query to enquire about the traffic situation prevailing in the city. Generally, the replies are given promptly. However, some complaints about not receiving any response from the Delhi Traffic Police could also be observed.

This provides the scope for two way communication between the Delhi Traffic Police and the general public. Such measures are often avoided by certain organizations, because they fear negative feedback from the public but it must be commended that the Delhi Traffic Police has braved this possibility and reaped very positive results since the number of abuses or complaints were not in very high numbers at all. Rather, the public seems to have appreciated the efforts made by the authorities to reach out to the people with the relevant information.

Screen shot of Delhi Traffic Police's Facebook Page

Though the reach of about 2.81 lakh people through Facebook is nominal if we take into consideration the fact that Delhi has over sixty lakh registered vehicles. Among the Traffic Police forces of the other metropolitan cities of the country, Kolkata and Chennai have lesser number of likes to their Facebook pages at 2.3 lakhs and 96,000 respectively. While Bengaluru Traffic Police has substantial presence with 4.9 lakh likes, Hyderabad Traffic Police has 3.3 lakh likes. Surprisingly, Mumbai's Traffic Police doesn't have an official Facebook page (as on 28th April, 2020). Let us have a comparative study of the Facebook penetration of the major Traffic Police forces within India and abroad to analyse how much of an impact the Delhi Traffic Police Facebook page has been able to make.

Facebook Page of a city traffic police (till April, 2020)	Number of likes
Kolkata Traffic Police	2.3 lakhs
Mumbai	No official Facebook page
Chennai City Traffic Police	96,446
Bengaluru Traffic Police	4.9 lakhs
Hyderabad Traffic Police	3.3 lakhs
Pune Traffic Police	1.3 lakhs

Comparison with the Facebook Pages of traffic forces of international cities

Facebook Page of a city traffic police (till April, 2020)	Number of likes
New York	No dedicated Facebook page for traffic management. (The official NYPD Facebook page has over 8 lakh likes)
London	No dedicated Facebook page for traffic management. The Metropolitan Police Service Facebook page has 2.4 lakh likes
Sydney (Traffic and Highway Patrol Command – New South Wales Police)	4.34 lakhs
Toronto (Traffic Services/ Highway Patrol)	3,214

* The above tables have been compiled as per the data available on the Facebook pages of the organizations mentioned in the table as on 28th April, 2020. It may also be

appreciated that the administrative mechanisms of different cities across the world vary from each other and therefore, such a comparison may not always be the appropriate indicator of new media usage or efficacy by a particular organization.

Twitter Handle

The official Twitter handle of the Delhi Traffic Police - @dtptraffic was launched simultaneously with its Facebook page in May, 2010. The page has over 1.2 million followers and close to two Lakh tweets have been sent from the handle so far. Much like its Facebook counterpart, about eight to ten tweets are sent out on an average every day updating the motorists about the traffic situation in the national capital.

Since Twitter allows tweets of only 280 characters, the messages are short and direct. The tweets are done simultaneously with Facebook posts and sometimes, if the information is voluminous, the Facebook links are also provided. In addition, photographs, videos about various events, seminars, workshops etc are also uploaded regularly. The tweets are generally of the following manner, "Traffic Alert Traffic is normal at DDU Marg".

While, the number of followers to the Twitter handle are much more than the number of likes on the Facebook page, the response from the followers are not in very high numbers. It seems that the Twitter handle is primarily used to get traffic updates from the Traffic Police rather than giving any feedback or making any complaints. Most service based agencies nowadays use Twitter to primarily convey their information and avoid two way communications.

**Screen shot of the Twitter handle of the
Delhi Traffic Police**

Unlike the Facebook Page, the following of the Twitter handle with over 1.2 million (12 lakhs) followers is pretty significant, though the number is still less than one third of the total number of vehicles plying in the city (approximately 60 lakhs). However, combining Facebook and Twitter, about 15 lakh people are using social media to get information about the traffic situation in the national capital, which is certainly a very encouraging number. Let us see, how the Twitter handle of the Delhi Traffic Police compares with the official Twitter handles of the traffic police forces of the other cities of the nation and some across the world.

Unlike Facebook, in case of Twitter, the Traffic Police forces of none of the other cities seem to have the kind of penetration and reach that Delhi Traffic Police has. While Mumbai does not have a dedicated twitter handle for traffic management, all other prominent Indian cities such as Kolkata, Bengaluru, Hyderabad, Chennai and Pune have separate twitter handles for disseminating traffic related information. However, all these twitter handles are reasonably well maintained and provide regular inputs to the people regarding traffic movement in their respective cities.

In the international scenario, most cities in the developed world do not have dedicated twitter handles for traffic management like in India. New York, London and Toronto do not have any traffic police handle as such however, their general police handles also share information about the major traffic developments. In Sydney, the Transport for NSW, the nodal agency there for traffic management maintains a twitter handle as well called @livetrafficSydney for traffic related updates. While, we must consider that different cities have varied traffic management mechanisms, we must also appreciate that the Delhi Traffic Police has taken a lead over many established traffic police forces of the developed world also in terms of utilizing the benefits of new media for reaching out to the citizens.

Twitter Handle of a city traffic police (till April, 2020)	Number of followers
Kolkata	48 thousand
Mumbai	No dedicated traffic police handle
Chennai	24.9 thousand
Bengaluru	5.9 lakhs
Hyderabad	67.6 thousand
Pune	87.8 thousand

Comparison with the Twitter handles of traffic forces of international cities

Twitter Handles of a city traffic police (till April, 2020)	Number of followers
New York	No Twitter handle
London	No Twitter Handle
Sydney	86.9 thousand (managed by Transport for NSW)
Toronto	No Twitter Handle

* The above tables have been compiled as per the data available on the Facebook pages of the organizations mentioned in the table as on 29th April, 2020.

Delhi Traffic Police Website

The website of the Delhi Traffic Police – www. delhitrafficpolice.nic.in, is an important ingredient of their public relations strategy. A continuous scroll on the home page of the site keeps sharing details about the areas in which traffic has been hampered. In addition, a lot of effort is made through the website to educate the visitors about the traffic rules and the rules for safe driving.

There is a dedicated section on road safety and education. In another section tiltled 'Be Road Smart', details about the high congestion areas, water logging prone locations, functioning of traffic signals are shared with the visitors. The 'Public Interface' section tells the visitors about the authorized parking areas, prepaid booths, mobile application usage etc.

The website has been designed in a specific manner to give the police force a humane impression. There is a separate 'services' section, in which it is clearly enumerated how to get a no objection certificate or a permission into the no entry areas. The 'Know Your Traffic Circle' link gives details of all the traffic circles along with the mobile numbers of the concerned Deputy Commissioners as well as the Assistant Deputy Commissioners.

Apart from the 'Traffic Updates' scroll, another scroll titled 'Traffic tips' also keeps running which gives information such as organization of 'lok adalats' for settling of pending cases etc. This apart, there are the usual sections generally found in all such websites such as the helpline numbers, photo gallery, notices sections. An 'FAQs' section has been provided on which all basic questions pertaining to traffic such as rules for obtaining NOCs, paying traffic related penalties, towing away of vehicles etc have been shared shared in a lucid manner.

Women's safety has been a matter of great concern for the national capital for a long time now. To make the women feel safer, a dedicated mobile application titled 'Himmat' has been created by the Delhi Police. Through the application, one can easily contact the police and relatives in case of any emergency. Though the 'Himmat' app is not directly connected with the traffic wing, but its links have been shared on the site as well, presumably to increase its popularity.

Another section with the name 'Traffic advisories/ diversions' shares information about the areas, where traffic diversions have been or are going to be put in place. Community involvement has also been given due importance. Details about the Traffic Training Park, formation of road safety clubs in schools have also been provided. A feedback section has also been provided.

The social media links for Facebook and Twitter are available on the bottom of the site facilitating the movement of the visitor directly to the social media sites for sharing of information.

Screenshot of the Delhi Traffic Police website

The site also performs well in comparison to the traffic police websites of the other major traffic police forces of the country. The Mumbai Traffic Police site – www.trafficpolicemumbai.maharashtra.gov.in, is also quite comprehensive but it seems more focused on showcasing its achievements rather than helping out the visitors. The 'Achievements' section is the most prominent with details of the number of cases handled, penalties imposed etc. The Kolkata Traffic Police's website – www.kolkatatrafficpolice. gov.in is also pretty detailed with its content and has more or less the same features as the Delhi Traffic Police website. The Chennai Traffic Police doesn't have a dedicated

website while the Bengaluru Traffic Police's website – www.
bangaloretrafficpolice.gov.in looks a bit cluttered with a lot
of phone numbers and links in on the home page, though it
scores well for providing conveninent links to its social media
handles. The tweets sent by the Bengaluru Traffic Police are
also displayed real time on the homepage. The website of
the Hyderabad Traffic Police – www.htp.gov.in is designed
on the pattern of a traffic junction, but it doesn't have much
new to offer in terms of content. It also displays the Twitter
feed of the Hyderabad Traffic Police's twitter handle.

Interestingly, four major traffic police departments of
prominent cities across the world – London, New York,
Sydney and Toronto did not have dedicated websites. In all
these cases, traffic related links were provided on the website
of the city police. The links were also mostly inadequate
in terms of providing real time traffic information to the
motorists.

WhatsApp service

The latest entrant to the bouquet of new media tools
employed by the Delhi Traffic Police is the WhatsApp
helpline service. WhatsApp is an internet based chatting
service, through which users can easily share photographs,
videos with each other. The messaging service currently has
over 1.5 billion active users worldwide and the number
will further increase further in the years to come. In a
city like Delhi, a majority of the motorists have access to
smartphones, which makes it very convenient for them to
post their complaints, queries, suggestions to the traffic
police authorities.

Introduced in October, 2014, the Delhi Traffic Police can be reached through the number 8750871493. According to media reports, Delhi Traffic Police received close to 85,000 complaints on the WhatsApp service till April, 2015. Out of these, over 7,000 complaints were found to be genuine and were settled by the Police authorities. The figures shared by the Traffic Police with the media genuinely proves that the service has been of huge benefit to the commuters in the city. There are many occasions when a motorist may not be able to call the traffic police on phone, but can easily leave a message on WhatsApp.

The Traffic Police authorities have been able to gauge the potential of this new medium in reaching out to the target audience and therefore, substantial manpower has been pressed into service to make the service a success. The WhatsApp service is available in both English and Hindi round the clock and an inspector and 25 traffic police officers monitor the complaints on a 24 hour basis. (The Press Trust of India report, 19th April, 2015)

Almost all other major traffic police forces across the country also have dedicated Whatsapp services. However, the researcher here couldn't find any other country around the globe where WhatApp is being used for traffic management. Many cities of the developed world such as London, New York, Sydney and Toronto were searched on the internet but no such information could be retrieved. Similarly efforts were also made to search for such services in the cities of the neighboring countries like Colombo, Dhaka and Karachi but no such initiative could be noticed. This also indicates that the police forces in India might be pioneers in utilizing such services for traffic management.

Helpline services

The most conventional among the new media tools employed by the Delhi Traffic Police are the telephone helpline services run by them. These services have been there for many decades and it can be debated whether they can be termed as 'new media' at all given the fact that they are not internet based and can be accessed from the traditional landline telephones as well. However, they have been included in the study since most helpline services around the world have been digitized and upgraded to the Interactive Voice Response Service (IVRS) based platforms.

However, it was observed that the two helpline numbers provided by the Delhi Traffic Police on their website – 0112584444 and 1095 were not very easily accessible. On most attempts made by the researcher, there was no response on these numbers or they couldn't be reached at all. When the numbers were picked, the response was polite and the relevant information was shared but the helplines do not function on the IVRS platform.

Mobile Application

The Delhi Traffic Police introduced a dedicated mobile application for traffic complaints and updates in May, 2014. This free application is available on Google store and can be easily downloaded on Android platforms. The application is available on the Windows and Apple based devices as well.

Mobile applications are downloadable content which allow the users to surf through relevant information even when the user is offline. In addition, the applications, popularly known as Apps also facilitate the transmission of updated information to the device on which it has been downloaded.

The mobile application of the Delhi Traffic Police is easy to use and has a number of features for the benefit of the users. The dashboard of the app has the following sections – Traffic Advisory, Traffic Alert, Taxi/Auto Fare, Complaints, Signal Fault, Towed vehicles, Emergency Contacts, FAQs, Offences and Lost report.

Therefore, the app is quite comprehensive and covers almost all aspects of the functioning of the Traffic Police. Traffic updates, details of taxi/ auto fares, signal faults, towing of vehicles, emergency contacts, lodging of lost reports can all be done through this application. The app sends regular traffic updates to the users in both English and Hindi. On an average, about six to eight updates are sent to users every day. However, it must be accepted that the app is just a good beginning. More features such as downloadable traffic awareness games, videos may be added. The overall look of the app with a deep blue background may also be improved and made more attractive.

The app, developed and maintained by the IT centre, Delhi Police headquarters, is about 3.3 megabytes in size and a bit slow for some devices having lesser capacity. However, once downloaded, it is quite effective with its updates. It has already been downloaded by close to one lakh users and the users have so far given it a very impressive rating of 4.2 out of five. Out of the 1,965 users who have reviewed it (as on 11th July, 2015), a very impressive 1,091 users have given it a perfect five while, 474 users have given four stars.

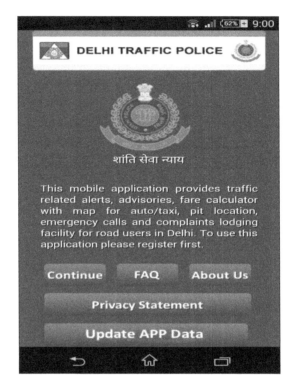

Screenshot of the Delhi Traffic Police Mobile App

The utility of the mobile applications has been realized by most of the traffic police forces across the country. Only with the exception of Chennai, all other major cities of the country such as Mumbai, Kolkata, Bengaluru and Hyderabad have started official traffic related mobile applications. All these applications are fed with basic traffic updates, emergency contacts, complaint numbers etc. Internationally, the trend of government created traffic apps does not seem to be very popular. For cities like London and Toronto, there are many excellent traffic update apps, but these have been developed by private companies. The

New York Police (NYPD) and Sydney Police (NSWP) have their official mobile applications, but these applications are mainly used for controlling crime rather than traffic. Closer home, Dhaka Police also has a mobile app but its not a specialized application for traffic management.

University of Delhi

The University of Delhi has substantial presence on the internet based platforms for communication, which we often refer to as 'new media'. Apart from a Facebook page, the university has an official Youtube channel, a website, an admission specific mobile application and of course a helpline number for students. The university also seems to have an account on the micro blogging site Twitter though it is not verified and has minimal following. The following are the details about the various new media tools used by the University of Delhi:

Facebook Page

The official Facebook page of the University of Delhi is quite popular among the students and their family members. It already has over 9.5 lakh 'likes' with substantial activity all year round. It regularly updates visitors about the many seminars, workshops and other such events taking place in the campus. The Vice Chancellor and other invited guests also conduct webinars from time to time and the links are made available. During the admission season, updates and details are also provided from time to time.

However, from an analysis of the Facebook page, it can be concluded that the university authorities do not intend to utilize the page to interact too much with the stakeholders. Rather they would prefer to use it to share details they are interested in sharing. As a result, some of the contemporary issues facing the university do not find a mention in the page. This intent of the university is also clarified through the disclaimer uploaded by them.

"Let's keep the comments civil, cordial and relevant to the topic, so that we can have this open space for all.

While the University shall take all possible care in ensuring the accuracy of the accuracy of the information that is uploaded on the site by the official University site Administrators, it shall not be responsible for any incorrect or incomplete information and the consequences of using such information. The university similarly shall not be responsible for any such information posted on this site by persons other than official site Administrators.

Rules to be followed:
Comments will be monitored.

Comments containing/linking any abusive material, personal attacks, profanity or spam will be deleted. The comments can't be used as ad space. So, please don't endorse, promote or solicit on behalf of a product or service.

Advertisements on this Facebook page are not endorsed or commissioned by the University of Delhi.

The page of our university aims to make information sharing even more quick and effective. Designed with the purpose of making the University processes as transparent as possible, it aims to provide the information relating to colleges & departments, libraries & services. You will find information on admissions & examination. It provides information on the achievements of our faculty members and their research interests. You can also get information about the upcoming events like workshops, events, conferences and lectures being held across the University as well." (https://www.facebook.com/UniversityofDelhi, 2015)

However, when the page was analysed again May, 2020, the above disclaimer could not be located.

**Screenshot of the Facebook page of the
University of Delhi**

In comparison it was found that none of the major government run universities in the major cities such as the Jawaharlal Nehru University, Delhi, University of Kolkata, the Annamalai University, Chennai or the Mumbai University had verified Facebook pages. Most of the private universities, in contrast have properly maintained social media presence. The prominent names such as Amity University, Lovely Professional University and Sharda University have Facebook as well as Twitter pages and social media is aggressively used to attract students towards them.

On the international front, it was observed that most of the universities of international repute world over have official social media presence. These pages have huge traffic and queries from all over the world. The Facebook pages of the University of Oxford and the Harvard University had queries from all corners of the globe and they were being addressed by a dedicated team on a regular basis. However, most of the universities in the Indian sub continent outside India did not have official presence on Facebook.

Name of the University	Number of 'Likes' on Facebook (as on 1st May, 2020)
University of Oxford	38 lakhs
Harvard University	55 lakhs
University of Melbourne	4.5 lakhs
Columbia University in the city of New York	4 lakhs
University of Minnesota	1.93 lakhs
University of Dhaka	6.3 lakhs
University of Karachi	No verified Facebook page

Youtube Channel

The official Youtube channel of the University of Delhi is called Univofdelhi. Dedicated Youtube channels can be utilized for sharing videos of seminars, symposia, lectures etc as well as video streaming of important events. For any educational institution, having a Youtube channel is a beneficial idea. However, the channel still seems in its initial stages without much activity.

As on May, 2020, the channel had about five hundred subscribers and a handful of videos had been uploaded. Therefore, obviously, the potential of the medium has not been utilized. In fact, social media presence can become rather embarrassing if not used properly. The Youtube link is provided on the home page of the university website, yet it is not verified. The university has faculty of great quality and many experts keep visiting to participate in many programmes. The entire academia could have benefitted at lot if their deliberations had been regularly updated on the channel.

**Screenshot of the Youtube channel of
the University of Delhi**

At the national level, most of the other major government run universities of the country do not have Youtube channels. Some universities such as the Annamalai University, Chennai, Hyderabad University do have some presence but they are not verified. In comparison again, the private universities such as Amity University and Sharda University have official Youtube channels where apart from the academic discourses, they also upload videos of student fests and concerts, which helps in attracting more students. On the international front again, most of the reputed universities had Youtube channels with large number of subscriptions and regular activity.

Name of the University	Number of 'Subscriptions' on Youtube channel (as on 2nd May, 2020)
University of Oxford	194,000
Harvard University	1.16 million
University of Melbourne	60,000
Columbia University	64,900
University of Minnesota	12,900
University of Dhaka	2,910
University of Karachi	No official Youtube Channel

The University of Delhi also has an Instagram page but that also is not very actively used.

University of Delhi website

The website of the University of Delhi – www.du.ac.in, does not quite look like a traditional website of a government run university. It is aesthetically designed and includes all the vital links conveniently on the home page, without cluttering the look. For example, during the admission seasons, it features important information such as the admission cut off lists prominently on the home page on the 'Latest' section. Similarly, other relevant information about the session ahead are displayed prominently.

Overall, the website is exhaustive and includes sections such as Academics, syllabi, research, libraries, amenities, alumni, administration, committees etc on the home page. All these sections again have a number of sub sections detailing various aspects of the functioning of the university. The Social Outreach section has details about the community centric activities that the university takes up.

A Lecture Series section has the links to the special lectures that are organized by the university. There is a link to the community radio station as well apart from other routine links such as tenders. Work with DU etc. The spotlight section has details of all the new developments that are taking place. It's similar to the 'What's New' section seen in many other sites. The home page also provides information about the two campuses of the university in north and south Delhi. Interestingly, during the Covid 19 pandemic in 2020, the website created a separate home page which opened first and provided all notifications regarding the pandemic and the change in the academic exercise because of the same.

There are two sections for the journalists. One is the 'Press Release' section, where the press releases and statements have been uploaded and the other is the 'In Media' section, where links to important news coverage about the university has been provided. This clearly shows that the university intends to utilize the website for maintaining good media relations as well.

The Research section is pretty exhaustive and covers a lot of vital details. There are dedicated links for the libraries,

The 'Alumni' section opens up to a separate site – www. alumni.du.ac.in which has details of the various eminent personalities who have passed out from the university. It lists out the global achievers, eminent leaders, judges, those in the corporate, civil/ foreign services, literary personalities, media-persons, sportsmen, academics etc. database forms are available where the alumni can also enroll if they desire.

Screenshot of the university website

The websites of the other prominent government universities of the nation – the universities of Mumbai, Calcutta as well as the Annamalai University, Chennai and the Jawaharlal Nehru University, Delhi were also studied thoroughly to compare the efficacy of the University of Delhi website. It was observed that the websites of the other universities were much more traditional in their look and were not as attractive as the website under study. The websites of some of private universities were also studied. It seemed that those websites were more focused on attracting new students rather than providing information related to all aspects of the functioning of the university.

However, the website has much to improve in comparison to the websites of the globally renowned institutions such as the University of Oxford or the Harvard University. These websites are beautifully designed with stories about the important research programmes of the students, the CSR activities, sports, cultural activities etc. Rather than looking like academic websites, these sites look like independent news portals with information about so many diverse activities – all of course related to the university.

Online Admission portal

For the first ever occasion, online admissions were introduced for the under graduate courses commencing in 2015. The online procedure, already available with many Indian and international universities was received very well by the students. Just after logging in to the University of Delhi website, link to the online site was provided. The ones interested to visit the university website could also do so by pressing the relevant link. A similar Post Graduate admission portal was also started.

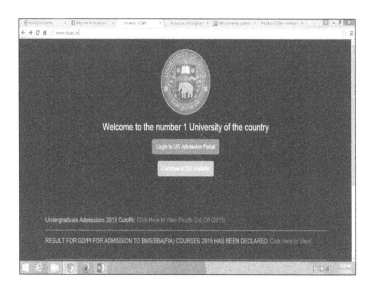

**Screenshot of the home page link to the
online admission portal**

Undergraduate Admission mobile application

In 2014, the University of Delhi launched a mobile
application on Android to help students aspiring to take
admission in the university. The app contained all relevant
information about the institution, its courses, important
dates etc. however, it may be added that there are many
privately designed mobile applications which are quite
comprehensive with their information about the admission
season. A search on the Google playstore shows at least eight
to ten similar applications which claim to have the necessary
information about the university.

The University of Mumbai also has designed a mobile
application for its students. The privately run Amity
University, with its app called Amizone, claims to be the

first ever university in India to design a mobile application for the students. (http://www.amity.edu/app/, 2015)

Helplines

The University of Delhi runs helpline services for the students from where important information about the admission procedure as well as other details can be sought. Two separate numbers with multiple lines – 155215 (without precode) and 011-27006900 can be reached by the students from Monday to Friday from 9 AM till 5 pm. During the undergraduate admission seasons every year, these helpline numbers receive approximately 300 calls every week.

Conclusion

The two case studies enumerated above certainly show that the public sector has adapted the infinite potential of social media. The social media channels used by these organizations have certainly helped them to devise a potent communication policy where brand building as well as grievance redressal are being addressed.

*The above information is based on the inputs gathered by the author during his doctoral research. Since this domain is very dynamic, the content available on the platforms discussed may undergo major changes from time to time.

Chapter 7

Case Studies in the
Indian Private Sector

As mentioned in the previous chapters, the adoption of new media tools was much faster in the Indian private sector in comparison to their government counterparts. With the gradual increase in the penetration of internet in the Indian society, the reliance on new media tools gradually increased. Now, many corporate houses invest more on their social media positioning than they do on conventional modes such as television commercials or print advertisements. Let us have a look at some products which carved a distinct niche for themselves with intelligent use of new media channels.

Fevicol

Fevicol, an adhesive brand from the Pidilite Industries is a household name in India. The brand name has almost become synonymous with the word adhesive over a period of time. Therefore, it is not so important to specify or advertise the quality of the products of this brand as such. But in a market, which is becoming increasingly competitive with many new brands making a foray, it is very crucial to continuously remind the consumers that Fevicol is the brand that they have historically been using, because it is the most reliable of all.

Therefore, we can notice that Fevicol's new media positioning is very interesting. Rather than discussing about the specific qualities of their product the campaign discusses how reliable Fevicol is in our daily requirements. The product's primary social media focus is on Facebook, where it has close to One Lakh Forty Thousand likes. However, its Twitter outreach is limited to only 7,800 followers.

Fevicol's Facebook Account

Fevicol's official Facebook account posts content largely promotional in nature every couple of days, which is not very frequent. However, the content is mostly witty and attracts a large number of likes from the visitors. For example, on 26th April, 2019, it posted the following creative.

It was a simple creative, which primarily induced the viewer to reverse the phone because the written content was turned upside down. The simple message that the material kept on the table would not fall down even if you turn the phone upside down would surely leave a smile in the face of the viewer. The creative neither was content heavy, nor had any detail on the specific product quality, yet it was such a massive brand establisher for Fevicol. The post garnered over 500 likes and 50 shares which is a very good number for such promotional content. One of the comments read, "Hats off to creative and marketing team. They deserve a great appraisal this time."

Similarly, on the occasion of Labour Day (1st May, 2019), they issued a very sweet post, which said that on this day even the legendary elephants, which are a part of the Fevicol logo deserved a break.

Fevicol's Twitter and Instagram Accounts

Fevicol's official Twitter account has little over 7,800 followers and the content is largely similar with that of Facebook. Their Twitter positioning does look a little inadequate given the fact that Twitter is generally considered a more dynamic medium than Facebook. However, it may also be added that in the Indian context, Facebook has more followers and better penetration especially in the interior areas beyond the metropolises. Twitter is largely used by a young audience, which may not use adhesives very frequently. However, Facebook has a more varied user base in comparison. Fevicol also has close to 25000 followers on its Instagram account and the content is largely the same. On Facebook, while the quality of the creatives is excellent which help them get great reactions, the response from Fevicol is minimal. This is one aspect where they can certainly make more efforts.

Fevicol's official website

Fevicol does not have a dedicated website of its own. However, it has a dedicated section on the corporate website www.pidilite.com. The corporate website is well designed with ample space given to all its products, their corporate social responsibility (CSR) activities etc. However, given the popularity Fevicol enjoys as a brand, it would be appropriate to design a dedicated website for it. There are also a bevy of products within the Fevicol brand. Therefore, there is sufficient scope for a separate website.

Durex

British origin condom brand, Durex from the Reckitt Benckiser group has an extremely witty new media presence with excellent brand positioning. Their Facebook account has over eleven million likes which would easily be among the highest among the products of this nature. Their Twitter account has over 27,000 followers. These numbers are significantly high given the fact that many users would be a little cautious about liking or following such products as the same would also reflect on their pages. @DurexIndia is the account name for their official Indian accounts. They have similar accounts for all major markets across the world.

Durex India's Facebook Page

Durex India's Facebook page is their most prominent presence on social media. With over eleven million likes, their posts also get great response from the users. However, they are not very regular with their posts. From their wall, it could be observed that they post some content or the other every alternate day or so. Almost all their posts get about a hundred shares and more than a hundred comments, which is a tremendously good number for a product of this nature. The social media response to Durex India's Facebook page also signifies how the average Indian user is coming out of the closet and discussing their sex related issues openly. The page is especially popular among youngsters. Most of the content posted by Durex is of the audio visual nature. While many of their posts are product specific and clearly lay down the qualities of the products, some are just fun creatives which are posted just for the engagement of the visitors.

They also position Durex as a fun product which identifies with a young and energetic target audience. For example, the creative below connects the product with the popular web series Game of Thrones. Such brand positioning connects immediately with the audience and influences their opinion in favour of a certain product or service.

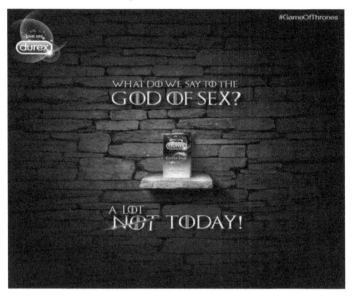

Similarly, in another post, they have designed their creative imitating the design of the Hollywood blockbuster series 'Avengers'. This coincided with the worldwide release of the last installment of the Avengers series – Avengers Endgame. There was tremendous buzz around the release of the movie and therefore this post garnered tremendous response. The post had an incredible 4.5 thousand shares and 3.2 thousand comments. Most of the creatives and audio visuals are designed for a worldwide audience and are displayed on their social media pages across the world. India specific content, however, is rather limited though they do post during India based events such as the major festivals like Holi and Diwali. Their Facebook page also has a 'shop now' option which leads the users to the Durex India website. It could also be noticed that despite the high amount of traffic on the page, there was very little interaction with the visitors who are commenting on the posts. This is probably one aspect on which Durex India can work.

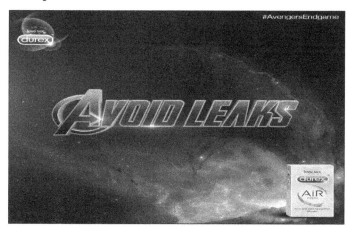

Durex India's Twitter and Instagram accounts

Durex India's Twitter handle @DurexIndia has close to 27,000 followers and the content posted by the handle is largely similar to their content on Facebook. However, as is the case with their Facebook, they interact very less with the visitors, who mostly share only appreciation for their brand.

On Instagram, Durex India has about 1.24 lakh followers and the content again is largely similar to the ones posted on Facebook and Twitter. However, to conclude it must be appreciated that the content posted by them is witty and connects easily with the target audience. There is a continuous effort to associate the product with the various developments happening across the world. This concept was made popular by Amul India in their advertising campaigns long before social media happened. Durex India is also carrying forward the same concept.

Durex India's official website

Durex's India website, www.durexindia.com allows the entry of only those above 18 years. However, the website, is attractive and meticulously lists the products that the brand sells. It is primarily an e-commerce website where all the Durex products are sold. They do not seem to have a corporate website which establishes their corporate identity. However, the group Reckitt Benckiser has a number of corporate websites and their positioning is well established.

Much like the two case studies mentioned in this chapter, there are many more instances where new media has been intelligently used to reach the target audiences more effectively. In fact, this space is so dynamic in nature that by the time, this publication goes to print, there would be many more such campaigns making rounds. However, the secret of success in these campaigns most certainly is clear messaging with lots of wit and humour.

*The figures and other details mentioned in the case studies may have undergone change during the time of publication of this book.

Chapter 8

PR Campaigns in the New Media Era

The nature of public relations campaigns in the new media era has undergone a sea change. There was a time when, an average public relations campaign would include components of mainstream media such as newspaper coverage, registering a presence in audio visual media platforms such as television and some presence on the internet.

However, with each passing day that picture is rapidly changing. In this chapter we shall analyse how PR campaigns are undergoing a sea change.

PR Campaigns in the 90s

In the 90s, even after the Indian economy had opened up to the tremendous potential of globalization, public relations campaigns largely revolved around coverage in the newspapers and other print publications such as periodicals. Television and radio still were secondary media and clients loved to read their names in the next day's newspapers. For example, for products such as consumer goods, clients would typically ask for coverage in a few leading mainstream dailies along with the few pink papers that operated.

After the events, PR professionals could be seen making rounds of media houses circulating copies of press releases. Press conferences and product launches were also not as glitzy and glamorous as they are today, because the visual appeal was confined to the photographs that the print shutterbugs would take. Doordarshan and All India Radio's coverage of business news was extremely limited and their patronage was not really a high priority area for the public relations professionals.

During the mid 90s however, the PR industry itself opened up. With a fast growing economy, the requirement of publicity for the various products and services that were hitting the market also emerged. Around the same time, television was finally emerging as a potent medium with multiple channels which telecasted only news items. Star News (operated by NDTV), Zee News were some of the initial players in the market.

With these developments, the nature of PR campaigns also started to change. Now print and electronic coverage were two different components of PR campaigns. This in many ways, triggered a paradigm shift in public relations planning as ever since the importance of print has consistently diminished over the last couple of decades.

As a result, now it became more important than ever before to make the product or the service visually appealing. Both the client and their PR handlers had to keep in mind that thousands of people were going to see the event on television. With the advancement of technology, OB vans became commonplace and television channels would often beam major events live, as a result of which now there was no scope whatsoever for any mistake or error.

Television brought in an element of immediacy to the news. Gone were the days when PR professionals could leisurely draft their press releases and circulate in the evenings. Now news was real time and had to disseminated real time for wide coverage.

PR Campaigns in the new millennium

As we approached the new millennium, the internet was gradually beginning to make an impact. However, PR campaigns largely revolved around the print and electronic media spheres. Rediff.com entered the news and entertainment space after registering its domain in 1996 and emerged as one of the first news and entertainment based websites in India. Yahoo, the US based web services provider also came up with an India specific website which carried news and views on India.

The online news scenario began to change gradually when mainline publications started their own news portals. The news agencies such as the Press Trust of India (PTI) also started their own websites as a result of which a lot of news content started getting generated online. By the year 2005, almost all major media houses, both print and electronic had their own news websites. However, in India, internet penetration was extremely low.

In addition, internet was still being accessed on computers and laptops unlike the present scenario where mobile phones are the main medium for accessing internet. With internet compatible smart phones being extremely expensive, people preferred to use their computers for surfing the net. However, surfing the internet on computers meant that people would access the net only for specific requirements. This fact deterred them from using the internet for accessing news. Unreliable connectivity and expensive internet charges were further deterrents for the users.

Because of the above mentioned reasons, PR professionals still preferred planning their campaigns around the print and electronic media though the digital space had started to make small inroads. A PR professional working with a top agency once said that, digital coverage was now being promised to clients as an additional attraction, often to win over others in the competition. Agencies would often try to woo clients by offering them some online coverage as well along with the main print and electronic coverage.

Social media had also now begun to make an entry. Orkut, a product launched by the Google stable was one of the first such platforms which gained massive popularity in India. Facebook and Twitter also entered the fray and created a buzz among the users. But their commercial potential was still not clear to the PR world. These platforms were still being looked at as youth centric forums largely confined to the urban areas.

Present Scenario

It would be extremely difficult to pin point an exact year when the digital started taking precedence over print and electronic as far as planning and executing public relations campaigns are concerned. However, it would suffice to say that the changes started appearing from around 2010, coinciding with the period when the social media started gaining prominence as a commercial tool and attracted millions of active users.

To start with, post 2010, digital coverage comprised about 20 percent of the total business pitch made by public relations agencies. Traditional media such as print publications and electronic media still comprised the bulk of the campaign plan.

Around the same time, social media platforms also started gaining great popularity. Facebook, for example added users all around the world cutting across ethnic, financial and gender divides. "Facebook has collected more users than there are followers of Christianity. More than 2.3 billion people use the service every single month. In some parts of the world, Facebook has become synonymous with the internet." (www.vox.com, 2019)

While Twitter filled up the micro-blogging space, many other social media platforms catering to different clientele emerged in the market. Instagram, Snapchat, Tinder, Linkdin etc caught the fancy of the users and today social media usage forms a bulk of the total internet use all over the world.

The distinct benefits of social media as a platform which could communicate a message directly to the target audience also further enhanced its utility. For decades, public relations practitioners had to rely on the journalists for dissemination of information. As mentioned in the earlier chapters, the journalists were the gatekeepers of information. PR professionals had no means to ensure that the message they intended to convey was eventually reaching the target audience. Therefore, this new innovation called social media emerged as a platform where there was direct interface between the client and the customer.

Presently, digital and print media occupy almost equal space in PR campaign plans. If the client asks for coverage in five mainline dailies, he also demands an integrated social media campaign with a certain number of likes and traffic. In case of campaigns for products related to the IT, Telecom or Automobile spheres, the share of digital media often is more than requirement for coverage in print. Since the clientele of these industries are generally heavy users of the internet, PR professionals also focus on the digital platforms. For example, a young professional planning to buy a smart phone would not check the newspapers to compare two models. Rather he would surf the net to compare the products and then take a decision. Television programmes dedicated to these spheres such as GSM Arena or Gadget 360 also have presence on the internet since many users watch these videos online.

The increase in the importance of digital media has also paved the way for a new breed of digital media PR experts, who provide only digital media solutions. These digital media experts provide solutions such as creation and maintenance of social media channels, implementation of online campaigns, development of mobile applications etc. They purchase likes and followers through commercial options provided by these channels. Without divulging on paper, these professionals also maintain troll accounts which are activated the moment the concerned brand faces any criticism or negative publicity.

Chapter 9

Change in Skill Sets for Public Relations Professionals

Till the 70s, there was practically no course specifically teaching public relations to the students. Gradually, public relations became a part of the study of Mass Communication and then even attained its own independent character as an academic discourse. Today, there are many post graduate diploma courses in advertising and public relations and even prestigious government institutions such as the Indian Institute of Mass Communication (IIMC) offer them.

Traditionally, these courses deal with crucial aspects of the profession such as the art of writing press releases, communication skills to reach out to the target audience, event management skills for organizing successful campaigns and so on. Even today, the nature of the curriculum of these courses hasn't changed so much.

However, in the last one decade, another expertise has become very important to become a successful public relations professional and that's the knowhow of working in the social media. Every prospective job seeker in the industry must acquire the necessary expertise to launch and run public relations campaigns through the social media for no public relations strategy can today be planned or executed without the use of the internet based platforms.

Every public relations professional today must know how to promote a product on social media. In addition, a clear idea about which social media site should be used to launch which product, what contents must the mobile application have to attract more downloaders must be there. Another important requirement is the idea about social media budgeting, that is knowhow about how more 'likes' and 'followers' can be generated by dealing with the concerned buying agencies and generating a buzz about the product concerned.

"Public relations professionals are known for their proactive attitudes, perseverance in pitching the media, a thick skin when it comes to rejection and the ability to build relationships, as well as their great oral and written skills. These are all important KSAs (Knowledge, Skills, Abilities) you need to be successful in public relations. However, social media has changed the way that public relations professionals approach the strategy and implementation of their public relations programs. Today, social media requires that we expand our KSAs for continued success in our public relations roles.

Social media causes us to think, prepare and act differently in our roles. Our knowledge has increased, and we're sharpening our skills and abilities. These expanded KSAs allow us to be more strategic to guide public interactions with our companies and to spearhead social media within our own organizations." (Breakenridge, 2014)

"Social media is reinventing the public relations playbook – and bringing with it the potential to raise the corporate profile of PR professionals. After all, PR professionals are among those who have pioneered the frontiers of social media.

To meet the challenge of their industries being "rebuilt around social engagement" – and to raise the profile of PR in the process – PR professionals must commit to lifelong learning, since the state-of-the-art for PR in social media is likely to continue evolving rapidly for years to come. (www. prnewswire.com, 2013)

New media has today emerged as a very potent tool for marketing as well, probably much more than a public relations tool, because of its instant reach and relatively lower expenditure. Therefore, to train the professionals dealing with marketing, innumerable digital marketing courses have emerged all over the country. These courses provide inputs in designing digital media, pitching products or services through them, social media usage, social media budgeting etc. Since public relations is a related field, these courses are much sought after today for public relations professionals as well.

These courses are available both online as well as through classrooms. Most of them are short term in nature starting from weekly modules to monthly, bi-monthly, six monthly and even yearlong courses. While some focus solely on digital marketing, some others also deal in details with the more creative aspects such as digital design. Many institutions, both government and private offer these programmes. The Indian Institutes of Management (IIMs) in Ahmedabad and Lucknow offer short term courses on digital media marketing. NIIT, the reputed computer training franchise also has many custom made courses with digital media as the main topic.

"Worldwide, the search interest in digital/online marketing courses has been in a steady up trend (or a secular bull market if you are a markets enthusiast) since the latter half of 2006. In India, the trend caught on late during the end of 2011 but since then, has seen a steady rise. With the growing internet penetration and social media popularity, this can only be expected to rise further.

To cater to the growing need for these courses, a number of companies and organizations have started various courses on Digital marketing. Digital marketing is a broad field and comprises various disciplines including Display ads, Search Engine Marketing(SEM) and Search Engine Optimization(SEO), Social Media marketing(SMM), Email marketing, Mobile Marketing and Affiliate Marketing. Each of these is a field in itself and there are field-specific courses being offered as well. Some of the courses come with certifications recognized by various bodies. Certification definitely cannot substitute for hands-on industry experience but, nevertheless, can add to the CV of a fresher making an entry into the field." (www. socialbeat.in, 2013)

Many other organisations such as Edukart, Digital Vidya, Digital Academy India, Market Motive etc offer these courses to thousands of professionals keen to further specialize and increase their expertise. Some of these institutions also run courses very specific to the requirements in public relations.

"Market Motive, co-founded in 2008 by American entrepreneur and Google Digital Marketing Evangelist Avinash Kaushik, provides online education and certification in six disciplines – Search Engine Optimization, Paid Search

Advertising, Social Media, Web Analytics, Conversion & Public Relations." (www.socialbeat.in, 2013)

While the marketing professionals might be more interested in promoting their product to the target audience, a public relations professional also has to ensure that the negative response of the target audience (if any) is immediately countered so that the traditional media doesn't feed from those responses. While now there are only short term courses dealing with digital media including social media, the time is not far when there will be full-fledged degree courses dealing with these issues since there will be further rapid growth in this sector. This is probably the single largest change in skill sets that has dawned upon the public relations industry ever since it matured into a full-fledged profession.

Chapter 10

New Media – The Emergence of a Full Fledged Industry in India

In this study, an effort is being made to evaluate the utility of new media as a tool of public relations. However, apart from its use as a medium of public relations, new media is today a full fledged industry with active roles in the marketing, news and entertainment sectors as well. Most of the new media tools are based on digital and internet based platforms and therefore, the terms 'new media' and 'digital media' are often used almost parrallely conveying the same meaning and connotation.

The digital media market of India has grown exponentially in the last few years. Online entertainment, news etc are playing the role of catalysts of the development of this sector. Social media, which is used extensively by the public relations industry also is increasing its presence with the rapid increase in internet penetration and the use of mobile devices such as smartphones and tablets.

The digital media market today boasts of over 220 million users and revenues of more than ₹ 25,000 crores. (www.business-standard.com, 2013)

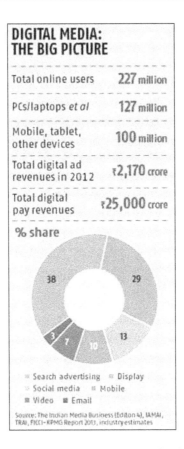

DIGITAL MEDIA: THE BIG PICTURE

Total online users	227 million
PCs/laptops *et al*	127 million
Mobile, tablet, other devices	100 million
Total digital ad revenues in 2012	₹2,170 crore
Total digital pay revenues	₹25,000 crore

% share

38 29 13 10 7 3

▪ Search advertising   ▪ Display
▪ Social media   ▪ Mobile
▪ Video   ▪ Email

Source: The Indian Media Business (Edition 4), IAMAI, TRAI, FICCI-KPMG Report 2013, industry estimates

Source: http:// www. business - standard.com/ article/ companies/ digital - media - picks - up - pace - in -india - 113071801152_1. html

Keeping in view the tremendous business potential of this sector, innumerable digital media companies have come up. While all news based, entertainment websites would come under the ambit of the digital media world, there are many digital media marketing organizations which are providing digital media solutions to both marketing as well as public relations companies. Most of these organizations offer integrated marketing as well as communications solutions to the clients.

Some of these companies are – Webchutney, Windchimes Communication, Sparrowi, Blue Digital, Media2win etc. All metropolitan cities have such agencies which specialize in creating content for social media and then communicating them to the maximum number of audiences. The Public Relations agencies now-a-days maintain digital or new media arms which primarily liaison with these agencies for the social media activities of their clients.

According to the digital media blog, www.soravjain. com, the number of digital media marketing organizations has increased from about 50 in 2011 to about 300 in 2015 indicating the exponential growth in this sector. "This number is growing now – we have about 300 Digital Marketing agencies in India and surprisingly most of them have varied clientele – which confirms Industries are finding digital marketing as an important integration to their marketing mix." (www.soravjain.com, 2015)

These companies provide custom made solutions to the clients, which include social media buying, campaign creation, monitoring and analytics, reputation management, customized app development, blogger services, search engine optimization etc.

"Apart from using traditional media, social media now is becoming an integral part of marketing strategy for almost all brands and personalities. Social media lets you connect and build one-to-one relation with your customers. However, it can also have a reverse impact if not used appropriately.

Most of the brands and personalities use atleast one of the social media platforms like Facebook, Twitter, Pinterest or Instagram. It helps you in building your brand as well as driving traffic to you website.

Social media and digital marketing agencies can become the best assistance to you in making seamless use of social media." (www.socialsamosa.com, 2015)

The Business of New Media as a Public Relations Tool

Right in the initial stages of planning a public relations campaign, the client is often asked about the number of people, he intends to reach through the new media tools. The strategists have to decide whether they want the social media campaign to be launched purely through personal contacts or through the buying of 'likes' and 'followers'. In case the concerned organization intends to launch its social media campaign without any buying of 'likes' or 'followers', the chances are high that the intended message would at best reach a few thousand people. However, in case the 'likes' and 'followers' are bought, they can be achieved according to the necessity or target set by the organization.

All prominent social media sites like Facebook and Twitter facilitate that. The algorithms of these sites are designed in such a way that specific posts or accounts can be exposed to more people on the basis of the payment made.

In addition, much like media buying agencies, social media buying agencies have also surfaced. These agencies tie up with the marketing or public relations companies and arrange 'likes' or 'followers' according to the requirement.

According to a public relations professional, these agencies functioning in Delhi generally charge about ten thousand rupees for arranging one lakh 'likes' or 'followers'. They deal with the social media website concerned and pitch the new post for the people.

Once a page, status, tweet or individual's profile is commercially pitched, it is displayed on the accounts of a large number of subscribers. In Facebook, there are links such as 'You may know', 'You may like' or the 'sponsored pages'. Similarly, in Twitter, there are links such as 'promoted by', 'sponsored by' etc. The pages, profiles etc are featured on those links giving them far more visibility then the other pages or profiles.

According to Mr. Sandipan Suklabaidya, a Delhi based public relations professional, once these are featured on the pages of the people, the chances of people liking them or following them increases manifolds. For Twitter, the probability of the promoted pages getting liked or followed is about 2.5 to three percent, while for Facebook, the rate is about five percent.

However, much more than the 'likes' and 'followers', the real reach of a page or a post is assessed through the number of 'shares' on Facebook and 'Retweet' on Twitter. In addition, the number of comments also decide whether a social media effort has really paid dividends. While a user may like a post or page just after a cursory or casual look, a share, a comment or a retweet would surely mean that he has read the post thoroughly. In the process, the possibility of garnering negative comments also exists. For tackling this issue, many organisations monitor the comments continuously and meticulously delete the abuses or complaints while many steadfastly reply to them. The new media experts in the public relations teams are assigned to monitor the presence on social media on a round the clock basis so that negative publicity or criticism can be avoided.

Another interesting way to promote a page is to get the celebrities to share them or retweet them. Most of the celebrities like cine actors, sportsmen have millions of followers on social media. If they agree to promote a certain post or page, immediately the message would reach millions of their followers. For example, for the promotion of the International Film Festival of India (IFFI), which is held in Goa every year, big cinema actors are often pulled in to comment or tweet about them. Even prominent film critics, directors are roped in for the job. On most occasions, it is done a gesture of cooperation, on many, money is also charged.

Nowadays, websites and mobile applications are also planned to disseminate the information to the target audience. While most organisations have their own websites, microsites are created to promote certain products, campaigns etc. Then, the links of these sites are shared on the social media platforms. The hits on the websites and the number of comments in the feedback sections are also effective indicators of the success or failure of a certain message that has been conveyed.

In case of mobile applications also, the number of downloads can be easily calculated which conveys whether the app has been received well by the target audience. Nowadays, for the service industry like insurance and online retail, apps have become a potent medium to not only push sales but also gauge whether a certain product has been well received. In order to increase the number of downloads, most organisations try to make apps for all the mobile platforms such as Andriod, Apple, Blackberry and Windows.

Another new media tool which is attracting the focus of the public relations practitioners is the practice of blogging. Initially, blogging was seen purely as non-commercial activity which allowed people to write their views, opinions and put on the web. But with the passage of time, now blogging has emerged as a full time profession with dedicated blogs on a range of topics. These blogs are so powerful, that negative feedback in them about a certain product can badly damage the business prospects since the information shared by these blogs are taken very seriously by the readers.

There are a range of blogs which review new mobile phones, electronic items, books, films, automobiles and so on. Over a period of time, these blogs have attained a lot of credibility, often more than the conventional news media. Therefore, public relations practitioners now also factor in their presence while planning public relations campaigns. Blogger meets are organized for niche bloggers who are given presentations about niche products and services and then they review them in their blogs. For example, www.indianautosblog.com, is an automobile related blog which extensively covers the nation's automobile industry. All major car launches, controversies are covered by the blogs which gets thousands of hits every day. In such a scenario, no public relations agency with an automobile client can afford to ignore this particular blog.

Similarly, www.bangaloreaviation.com, is a popular aviation sector blog which reports in details about the proceedings in the aviation sector. All the sectors have such dedicated blogs which have tremendous readership and the benefit of reaching out to them is that through them, the organisations can directly reach the customer base because, these blogs would be read by only specific readers and not random readers as may be the case with traditional media. Influencers are a new breed of 'celebrity social media users' who are followed by thousands of people. The following sometimes, exceeds millions as well. Therefore, when they endorse any product or service, it immediately attracts a lot of attention. Influencer Marketing is the new age fad of communicators today. Worldwide, influencer marketing is considered an important component of all PR campaigns.

In addition, some more new age methods are being adopted to take the message more effectively to the target audience. Search engine optimization is one of them. Now-a-days, it is common practice to search for certain information on the search engines like Google. In order to reach out to the maximum number of people through Google before the other contenders on the web, the public relations planners go for search engine optimization. That is, the content developers of the websites, social media posts are directed to develop the content in such a way that the weblink features prominently on the searches made on the search engines.

For example, if a web content is being developed for a new sedan car entering the market, the crucial key words expected to be used while searching online for such a product such as sedan, new, car, mileage, comfort etc should be used in the web content in such a manner that whenever a search is done about such products on the net, the concerned web link emerges on the top of the search ahead of the other similar links.

Geo targeting is another new age tool which is now being used widely in India. Though more of a marketing or even advertising tool, geo targeting is done to identify the location of the user and provide location relevant data to him. This is done by either determining the physical location of the user or through the locations searched by the user. For example, if a user searches for airline tickets repeatedly between Delhi and Silchar, then geo targeting will help identify the person and feature advertisements of travel booking websites with fares of this route. This is not a public relations tool as such but is used for reaching out to the target audience never the less.

Chapter 11

The New Media Bubble?

In the preceding chapters, we have discussed how new media has emerged as the primary tool for communication across the world. We have also analyzed how public relations practitioners are modifying their communication strategies to accommodate digital media platforms. The access and reach that these platforms are promising is indeed staggering and therefore, it is not at all surprising that communication strategies are being realigned in accordance with these new platforms.

However, with the passage of time, the new media world is also gradually maturing. The initial days of euphoria and excitement are giving way to a period of hard core analytics. Communication experts are trying to analyse whether, the numbers that these digital platforms actually promise to deliver are correct or not. Many from the traditional schools of communication are now actually asking whether this whole new media world is a bubble, which will eventually burst and the world will go back to the methods which have been in use for decades.

There are multiple dimensions to this challenge. At the start of the decade of the 2010s, when data penetration and speed was increasing at a rapid rate across the world, many established media houses as well as new start ups identified the digital media as a potent medium for disseminating information. It was widely believed that these platforms would gradually take over from traditional media as the main source of information. While, reliance on digital media for news has indeed increased manifolds and traditional media platforms, especially print media are facing an existential crisis, it is also true, that these digital media houses have failed to adequately monetize the potential.

The advertising opportunities through these online platforms are tremendous. However, the rates across the world are still extremely low. The online audience has become accustomed to reading online content for free and therefore, is not exactly forthcoming to pay for the same services they have enjoyed for free for years.

"Recent bad news for a number of digital-born news outlets (including BuzzFeed, HuffPost, Mashable, and Vice) is a symptom not only of the intense competition for attention and advertising online, but also of a digital content bubble where most news providers continue to operate at a loss — losses that cannot be sustained indefinitely.

So far, the largest digital-born publishers have been sustained by investors, some of whom may be losing their patience. Legacy media outlets have used their offline revenues to bankroll investments in online operations that are still often not profitable on their own. Smaller digital-born operations have started out with money from their founders or philanthropic backers, but many are struggling to break even.

More than 20 years into the rise of digital media, it seems clear that the content bubble will eventually burst unless more robust business models are found. Investors' high hopes and dwindling legacy revenues won't sustain digital news forever." (Nielson R. K, 2017)

Almost all leading publications in the United States, Europe have now put a price tag on the online content that they make available. However, in India, the scenario is still very different. Almost none of the online content providers are charging for the news they disseminate.

Journalists working with the online news portals such as The Print, Scroll, The Wire confide that time is still not ripe for their publications to charge for the content as the Indian audience is not ready for it. Therefore, many of these publications are struggling to make substantial profits. The advertising tariffs of these portals are still way lesser than the mainstream media like television and print. While a lot of online advertising is taking place, it is still not considered the main source of publicity, especially keeping a pan India audience in mind.

Similarly, the social media domain also has its share of uncertainties. Mark Zuckerberg and his ilk may have invented these media as tools for communication but now all social media giants have identified the business potential that these platforms hold. Therefore, gradually the algorithms of these platforms are becoming complicated. In other words, now, if you want your message to reach a large number of people, you must pay for it.

For example, on Facebook, an intended message initially would reach less than 10 percent of the desired audience if the whole campaign is done for free. There are multiple price slabs for purchasing likes and taking the post to a larger audience. Other prominent social media channels like Instagram and Twitter also have similar arrangements in place.

"As of late 2019, average reach for Facebook posts was down by 2.2%, meaning that brands could reasonably expect their posts to be seen by about 5.5% of their Page's followers. Big brands with massive follower counts can expect even lower averages.

It's true that the Facebook algorithm isn't the only factor that affects reach—there are others at play, like Facebook's continued growth—but it's definitely one of the most important factors. Which means marketers who don't stay up to date may have a tougher time getting their content in front of their audience's eyeballs." (Cooper P, 2020)

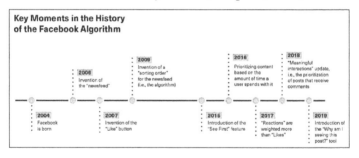

* www.hootsuite.com

In addition, new studies are now emerging which indicate that even if you 'purchase' a certain number of likes or followers, it is not necessary that the message would actually reach the intended target audience. A huge number of these accounts or handles are often 'bots', which are operated by computers and do not belong to original human beings. Even in cases of many celebrities, whose following may have grown organically because of their popularity and mass appeal, it was later found that many followers were actually fake and those human beings did not exist in reality.

For example, Shield Square, a start up with offices in India and the United States had said back in 2017 that many Indian celebrities such as Amitabh Bachchan and Virat Kohli had more 'fake' followers on Twitter than the real ones. In January, 2018, Amitabh Bachchan complained to Twitter that his followers had suddenly decreased. In fact he lost more than four lakh followers in a matter of days. He even threatened to leave the platform altogether. Other prominent actors like Shah Rukh Khan and Salman Khan also lost more than three lakh followers each. This happened after Twitter decided to remove accounts it deemed suspicious or fake.

These figures cast a major doubt on the reach and appeal that social media promises to provide. The entire world of public relations and advertising relies on data for planning its campaigns. In the initial years of social media, the data and direct reach that it promised seemed like its greatest assets. However, with the passage of time, as these platforms are maturing, doubts are emerging about their efficacy.

"Follower factories or click farms are springing up in India, China, Bangladesh, the Philippines and East European countries at a fast clip.

In November 2016, Facebook had disclosed that it had up to 60 million automated or bot accounts, double its previous estimation. By some accounts, more than 45 million of Twitter's reported active users are bots, and in India, too Twitter is littered with bots." (Laghate G, 2018)

In the last chapter, we discussed how 'influencers' had become major drivers in the social media scene, how many such influencers were actually influencing the choices made by the consumers. However, many of these influencers also are apparently purchasing their following and are presenting grossly bloated figures to the corporates who are interested in roping them in for the promotion of their products and services.

"Consumers are becoming more skeptical towards brands and their advertisement. Now the same is happening with influencer marketing. It is no secret anymore that influencers make quite a good business with promoting brands online. Thus, consumers start to question these promotions. They ask for more influencer authenticity and real-life presentation instead of 'fake' promoted posts." (Kandel, 2018)

Many cases have come to light in the last few years where, influencers have been found to have enhanced their following by having bots, which are basically computer generated accounts, that interact like real human beings on social media platforms. Various influencer marketing conferences across the world have time and again deliberated to find out ways and means to tackle this menace and eliminate any such unfair trade practice.

"Jess (not her real name) is a U.K.-based fashion influencer with 230,000 Instagram followers. She worked with 22 different brands in 2018 and charged $1,000 per post.

Those brands didn't realize that 96 percent of Jess's engagement is fake, the result of a bot farm she allegedly paid for engagement: $2 for every 1,000 likes, comments or shares. That means that each company Jess worked with likely wasted up to $960.

It's called "influencer fraud," a practice spawned after the digitalization of influencer marketing -- the latter of which has, in one iteration or another, been around for hundreds of years. Prominent online personalities purchase fake engagement via bots -- pieces of software designed to automatically like, comment and share social media posts. The other route is to join a community of real users that allows people to "trade" engagement back and forth (e.g., commenting on or liking 250 posts from others in the community to receive 250 comments or likes on your own posts)." (Field H, 2019)

"Fake influencers can either be bots, or real people who artificially boost their following and engagement by paying for it. The goal is to create accounts that, on the surface, may be of interest to advertisers, but fundamentally, do not influence many people.

Despite the efforts of platforms to suspend fake influencers, no one escapes the deception: not even the biggest brands! According to a recent North Group Points study, brands like Ritz-Carlton, Pampers and Magnum have invested heavily in campaigns involving artificial influencers." (Williams H, 2018)

Therefore, there is renewed stress now on ensuring that the influencers who are being roped in to promote certain products or services actually have the following they claim in their portfolios.

In light of the factors enumerated in this chapter, many experts have opined that the new media burst that we are witnessing today is like a bubble. It has expanded and spread its tentacles far and wide alright, but it may not stand the test of time. The main factors behind this reasoning are as follows:

a. **Unreliability of data:** Over a period of time, it has become apparent that data, which was considered the greatest strength of new media may well be its greatest weakness as well. The proliferation of computer generated accounts on all social media platforms have created a crisis, where advertisers, public relations professionals and marketers cannot rely on the data that is available to them. Many communication strategists are turning back to the good old data collection methods such as sample surveys conducted on ground to sell their products or services.

b. **Limited commercial possibilities for online media:** While a new breed of social media celebrities have emerged who are successfully monetizing their presence on various platforms such as YouTube, Facebook and Twitter, various online media houses have failed to generate sufficient revenues to keep their businesses going. In the developing world, especially in a country like India, the consumer is still not willing to pay for the online content they read or follow as a result of which the commercial prospects become limited.

However, to conclude, we may say that internet as a medium is here to stay. Its penetration across the world, including in the developing economies such as India, has been absolutely phenomenal in the last few years. India has the cheapest mobile data rates in the world and today almost every phone owner irrespective of social or economic hierarchies has access to internet. Online shopping has also proliferated like never before and India is one of the largest markets for online retail giants like Amazon. Therefore, the potential of all media which are internet based are infinite.

As the market matures and corporates find more reliable means to access the authenticity of data, the role of new media as a tool of public relations as well as advertising will only get further strengthened. Many agencies are already available in the market now which can access the reliability of data. They can also check the actual reach of the influencers who claim to have a large following. The role of social media platforms as purely economic entities is now well established and most communication strategies are being made with this in mind. Therefore, to suggest that, the new media domain is a bubble which will fail the test of time is inaccurate. However, we may agree to the fact that 'new media' in itself is a broad term and its nature will evolve with each passing day.

Bibliography

New Media – A View of the Studies Already Conducted

1. Socha, B. and Eber-Schmid, B. (2012), What is New Media, http://www.newmedia.org/what-is-new-media.html.
2. Kote, J. (2020), What is New Media, https://www.snhu.edu/about-us/newsroom/2020/02/what-is-new-media
3. Michaelian, B. (2012), New and Social Media, Is There a Difference and Does It Matter, http://www.worksmartmompreneurs.com/blog/socialmedia/new-and-social-media-is-there-a-difference-and-does-it-matter/
4. FAD Research (2006), Changing Media, Changing Roles: New Media Comes of Age, pp 4.
5. Larabie, C. (2011), A Reflection on the Role of New Media – From Peer-to-Peer to Protest, The McMaster Journal of Communication 2011, Volume 7, Issue 1, pp 2-3.
6. Aday, S, Farell, H, Lynch, M, Sides, J, Freelon, D (2011), New media and conflict after the Arab spring, United States Institute of Peace, pp 3-4.

7. Praeli, Y.S, (2011), New Media and the Freedom of Press, Reuters Institute For The Study Of Journalism, Oxford University (Electronic Version - https:// reutersinstitute.politics.ox.ac.uk/about/news/item/ article/new-media-and-freedom-of-the-press.html).

8. McAllister, S. and Taylor, M. (2007) Community college web sites as tools for fostering dialogue: Public Relations Review [Electronic version], pp. 230–232.

9. Hoggatt, L (1999), New Media Technology, School of Mass Communication and Journalism, San Jose State University, pp 1.

10. Hallahan, K., (2004) Protecting an organization's digital public relations assets, Public Relations Review, Vol. 30, pp. 255-268.

11. https://www.vitispr.com/blog/benefits-of-social-media-in-public-relations/, accessed on 06.04.2020 at 2:05 pm

12. Alfonso, G.H. & Smith, S. (2008). Crisis communications management on the web: how internet-based technologies are changing the way public relations professionals handle crisis. Journal of Contingencies and Crisis Management, 16(3), 143-153.

13. Porter, L, Sweetser, K and Chung, D (2009), Blogosphere and Public Relations, Emareld Journal of Communications, Vol. 13, No. 3, pp 250-51.

14. Porter, L, Sweetser, K and Chung, D (2009), Blogosphere and Public Relations, Emareld Journal of Communications, Vol. 13, No. 3, pp 261.

15. Gordon, J. (2011) Short & Sweet: The Whys and Hows of Twitter for Communications Professionals: www.fanton.com, pp 5.

16. Horton, J (2009), "PR and Social Media", www. http://www.online-pr.com/Holding/PR_and_Social_media.pdf, pp 1.

17. Smith, B (2011), Why Social Media is the New Public Relations, FixCourse Newsletter, pp 3.

18. Thomas, V. (2012), How is Social Media Evolving PR, www.pitchonnet.com, http://pitchonnet.com/blog/2012/11/30/hows-social-media-evolving-pr

19. 'The Importance of Social Media in Public Relations' (2012), www.maximisesocialmedia.com.

20. 'Vodafone India: Most Engaging Facebook Page for October 2012' (2012), www.socialsamosa.com.

21. Ningthoujam, P. (2009) Use of New Media tools: www.indiaprblog.com.

22. Bhatt, L. (2009), Financial Express, New Delhi edition.

23. 'A Conversation with PR 2.0 Guru Diedre Breakenridge, www.text100.com, accessed on 21.12.2012 at 1000 hrs.

Chapter 1

1. Bhatt, S.C (2000), Press Information Bureau: History, Evolution and Future, pp 1

2. Gersten. D, Heidi Cohen Actionable Marketing Guide, www.heidicohen.com, 2011

3. https://www.adgully.com/pr-industry-in-india-grew-12-to-reach-rs-1-600-cr-in-2019-prcai-report-90373.html, accessed on 06.04.2020 at 2:46 pm.

4. Banerjee, P. (2017), Inception of PR in India: www.prmuseum.org

Chapter 2

1. Socha, B. and Eber-Schmid, B. (2012), What is New Media, http://www.newmedia.org/what-is-new-media.html.

2. home.web.cern.ch, 2015 accessed on 22.06.2015 at 23 hrs.

3. Peter, I., The History of Email, www.nethistory.info, 2011 accessed on 23.06.2015 at 2115 hrs.

4. Clement, J. (2020), https://www.statista.com/statistics/272014/global-social-networks-ranked-by-number-of-users/, accessed on 10th April, 2020 at 12:44 PM.

5. www.monitor.icef.com, 2012 accessed on 23.06.2015 at 2245 hrs.

6. Venkatesh, G. (2019), https://www.thehindubusinessline.com/info-tech/social-media-start-ups-betting-big-on-non-english-speakers/article26431538.ece, accessed on 13th April, 2020 at 11:10 AM.

7. https://www.addthis.com/blog/2019/06/06/most-popular-social-media-platforms-around-the-world/#.XpVLnkAzbIU, accessed on 14th April, 2020 at 01:55 PM

8. http://www.engadget.com/2007/01/09/the-iphone-is-not-a-smartphone/ accessed on 25.06.2015 at 2210 hrs.

9. Bates S., A History of Mobile Application Development, 2014

Terms and Abbreviations – Chapter 2

1. *** DARPA - Defense Advanced Research Projects Agency (DARPA)** is an agency of the United States Department of Defense responsible for the development of emerging technologies for use by the military.

2. *** ARPANET - Advanced Research Projects Agency Network (ARPANET)** was the first wide-area packet-switching network with distributed control and the first network to implement the TCP/IP protocol suite.

Chapter 3

1. https://timesofindia.releasemyad.com/tariff/Times-of-India-Display-Advertisement-Rate-Card, accessed on 18.04.2020 at 11:21 AM

2. http://www.davp.nic.in/Em_rcav.html, accessed on 21.06.2015 at 01 hrs.

3. https://twitter.com/PMOIndia, accessed on 15.04.2020 at 0200 hrs.

4. https://www.statista.com/topics/2157/internet-usage-in-india/, accessed on 16th April, 2020 at 01:50 PM

5. http://www.iamwire.com/2015/01/rise-internet-penetration-changing-face-digital-india/108808, accessed on 23.07.2015 at 1810 hrs.

6. https://www.internetworldstats.com/top20.htm, accessed on 16th April, 2020 at 04:38 PM

7. https://economictimes.indiatimes.com/tech/internet/ internet-users-in-india-expected-to-reach-500-million-by-june-iamai/articleshow/63000198.cms, accessed on 30.04.2018 at 2230 hrs.

8. http://centerac.com/social-media-the-game-changer-of-lok-sabha-elections-2014, accessed on 24.06.2015 at 2235 hrs.

9. http://www.augure.com/blog/communication-campaigns-2014-2-20141218 accessed on 24.06.2015 at 23 hrs.

10. http://www.socialsamosa.com/2013/12/25-best-indian-social-media-campaigns-2013/, accessed on 24.06.2015 at 2330 hrs.

Chapter 4

1. Report on Internet Banking (2001), https://www. rbi.org.in/scripts/PublicationReportDetails.aspx, accessed on 21.06.2015 at 1000 hrs.

2. http://india.gov.in/e-governance/national-e-governance-plan, accessed on 23.07.2015 at 1830 hrs.

3. Digital India PDF document, 2015

4. www.digitalindia.gov.in/content/about-programme, accessed on 24.07.2015 at 1245 hrs.

Chapter 5

1. https://www.firstpost.com/business/90-indian-brands-spend-15-annual-marketing-budget-social-media-2168495.html, accessed on 05.07.2018 at 12.50 hrs.

2. https://yourstory.com/2018/01/10-interesting-things-happening-indias-mobile-app-universe/, accessed on 09.07.2018 at 11.25 hrs.

3. Steup, M. 2018, https://www.messengerpeople.com/messaging-apps-in-india/, accessed on 24th April, 2020 at 15:10 PM.

4. Kudritskiy, I. 2019, What is WhatsApp Business?, https://rocketbots.io/blog/whatsapp-business/, accessed on 24th April, 2020 at 15:28 pm.

5. Kudritskiy, I. 2019, What is WhatsApp Business?, https://rocketbots.io/blog/whatsapp-business/, accessed on 24th April, 2020 at 15:35 pm.

Chapter 6

www.Facebook.com, www.twitter.com, www.instagram.com, www.delhitrafficpolice.nic.in, www.du.ac.in, www.alumni.du.ac.in and websites of various educational institutions across the world were accessed multiple times by the author from 2010 till 2020.

Chapter 7

www.Facebook.com, www.twitter.com, www.instagram.com, www.pidilite.com, www.durexindia.com were accessed multiple times by the author from 2010 till 2020.

Chapter 8

1. https://www.vox.com/2019/2/4/18203992/facebook-15-year-anniversary-user-growth, accessed on 01.08.2019 at 14:30 hrs.

Chapter 9

1.   Breakenridge, D. (2014), Social Media skills and abilities, http://www.prsa.org/jobcenter/career_resources/resource_type/tools_tactics/social_media/, accessed on 16.07.2015 at 21 hrs.

2.   http://assets2.prnewswire.com/documents/wp_Mastering_Public_Relations_in_Social_Media.pdf, accessed on 16.07.2015 at 2115 hrs.

3.   http://www.socialbeat.in/2013/12/09/top-10-digital-marketing-courses-india/, accessed on 16.07.2015 at 2145 hrs.

Chapter 10

1.   http://www.business-standard.com/article/companies /digital-media -picks-up-pace-in-india-113071801152_1.html, accessed on 21.07.2015 at 1315 hrs.

2.   http://www.soravjain.com/indian-social-media-digital-marketing-agencies, accessed on 21.07.2015 at 1325 hrs.

3.   http://www.socialsamosa.com/2014/03/list-social-media-digital-marketing-agencies-india/, accessed on 21.07.2015 at 1345 hrs.

Chapter 11

1.   https://www.niemanlab.org/2017/12/is-the-digital-content-bubble-about-to-burst-for-some-of-the-publishers-chasing-the-broadest-scale-maybe, accessed on 30.03.2020 at 11:18 am.

2. h t t p s : / / w w w . f o r b e s . c o m / s i t e s / f o r b e s communicationscouncil/ 2018/ 05/02/the-case-for-brand-authenticity/ #5bd6057c6530, accessed on 29.03.2020 at 12:15 pm

3. https://blog.hootsuite.com/facebook-algorithm/, accessed on 31.03.2020 at 11:49 am

4. https://www.entrepreneur.com/article/331719, accessed on 29.03.2020 at 12:29 pm.

5. https://economictimes.indiatimes.com/tech/internet/ shadow-of-bot-followers-and-fake-likes-mars-social-media-influencers/articleshow/64674668. cms?from=mdr, accessed on 31.03.2020 at 12:16 pm.

6. https://www.meltwater.com/uk/blog/influencer-fraud/, accessed on 29.03.2020 at 12:56 pm

www.ingramcontent.com/pod-product-compliance
Lightning Source LLC
Chambersburg PA
CBHW051054050326
40690CB00006B/714